Gamer Dad: Keeping Up With Modern Gaming While Still Loving the Classics

Jack Lawson

Book Structure & Chapter Breakdown

Introduction: You Never Stopped Being a Gamer

- A look back at growing up in the 8-bit and 16-bit eras
- Why gaming is still a great hobby for adults
- How gaming has changed (and how it hasn't)
- Ditching the guilt: Yes, you have time to game

Part 1: Retro Gaming – Keeping the Classics Alive

- **Chapter 1: The Greatest Games You Grew Up With**
  - The most iconic titles from the '80s and '90s
  - Why these games still hold up today
  - Hidden gems you might have missed
- **Chapter 2: Building a Retro Gaming Setup in 2025**
  - The best ways to play old-school games on modern TVs
  - Original hardware vs. emulation vs. mini consoles
  - The ultimate retro gaming accessories
- **Chapter 3: Collecting and Restoring Classic Games**
  - Where to find classic games without overpaying
  - How to restore and maintain old cartridges, discs, and consoles
  - Building your dream gaming room

Part 2: Gaming with Your Kids

- **Chapter 4: Bonding Over Video Games**
  - Why gaming is a great way to connect with kids
  - The best modern games for co-op and family play
  - Introducing your kids to retro games (without them rolling their eyes)
- **Chapter 5: Managing Screen Time Without Ruining the Fun**
  - Striking the balance between gaming and real life
  - Setting gaming rules that actually work
  - How to encourage creativity and learning through gaming

Part 3: Modern Gaming for the Gen X Gamer

Introduction: You Never Stopped Being a Gamer

If you're reading this, chances are you grew up blowing into NES cartridges, feeding quarters into arcade machines, or spending hours perfecting your skills on *Street Fighter II*, *GoldenEye 007*, or *Gran Turismo*. Maybe you had the thrill of unpacking a brand-new PlayStation or spent weekends at a friend's house, taking turns on *Contra* until you ran out of lives. Gaming wasn't just a hobby—it was part of growing up.

But somewhere along the way, life happened. Careers, mortgages, kids, and responsibilities took over, and gaming got pushed to the side. Now, you might look at today's gaming world and feel like an outsider. Maybe your kids are playing *Fortnite*, *Minecraft*, or whatever the latest online sensation is, and you have no idea what's going on. Perhaps you've walked into a GameStop recently, stared at the shelves, and realized you don't recognize most of the titles anymore. You might even wonder: *Am I too old for this?*

Let me stop you right there—**you're never too old to be a gamer.**

The truth is, gaming has evolved, but so have we. As Gen X gamers, we were there for the birth of home consoles, the rise of the arcade scene, the golden age of RPGs, and the dawn of online multiplayer. We have a unique perspective that younger generations don't—we've witnessed gaming transform from a niche pastime to a global entertainment giant. The trick is learning how to navigate this new world of gaming while still staying true to what we love.

That's where this book comes in.

What This Book Is (And What It Isn't)

This isn't a deep dive into gaming history, nor is it a hardcore strategy guide. It's not meant for esports professionals or Twitch streamers. Instead, this book is for guys like you—dads, casual gamers, retro enthusiasts—who want to reconnect with gaming in a way that fits your life today.

In these pages, we'll explore:

- **How to relive the classics** without spending a fortune on vintage hardware
- **Modern gaming trends explained in plain English** (so you won't feel lost when your kid asks about "crossplay" or "battle passes")
- **The best games for busy dads** who can't commit to 100-hour campaigns
- **How to bond with your kids through gaming** (without embarrassing yourself too much)
- **The world of retro collecting, emulation, and arcade restoration** for those who want to take nostalgia to the next level
- **How to navigate online gaming without dealing with toxic players or endless microtransactions**

Most importantly, this book will remind you that gaming is meant to be **fun**—not a chore, not something you "grow out of," but a lifelong passion that evolves along with you. Whether you're looking to fire up an old favorite, discover new games, or just understand what the heck your kids are playing, this book will help you find your place in the gaming world again.

So grab your controller, and let's dive in. Because once a gamer, always a gamer.

Chapter 1: The Greatest Games You Grew Up With

If you grew up in the '80s and '90s, you witnessed one of the most exciting periods in gaming history. It was an era of pixelated platformers, side-scrolling beat 'em ups, and arcade showdowns where every quarter mattered. It was a time when couch co-op was king, cheat codes were sacred knowledge, and renting a game for the weekend meant you had two days to beat it before returning it to Blockbuster.

But here's the thing—many of those games **still hold up today**. Unlike some modern games that rely on massive open worlds and constant updates, classic games were designed with tight mechanics, addictive gameplay loops, and a simplicity that made them instantly fun. In this chapter, we'll take a nostalgic (but practical) look at some of the most iconic games of our childhood, why they're still great, and a few hidden gems that might have flown under your radar.

The Most Iconic Games of the '80s and '90s

These are the titles that defined a generation—the ones that kept us glued to our screens, arguing over who got the next turn.

Super Mario Bros. – The Game That Defined a Generation

In the mid-1980s, video games weren't new, but *Super Mario Bros.* changed everything. It wasn't just a game—it was *the* game. It turned living rooms into arcades, created legends on the playground, and made Mario the most recognizable character in gaming history. But beyond the simple act of running, jumping, and saving a princess, *Super Mario Bros.* had something special—it had **secrets**.

The Playground Was Our Internet: How Secrets Spread in the '80s

Today, if you want to find a hidden level or special trick in a game, you just Google it or watch a YouTube tutorial. Back in the '80s? **Secrets were currency.**

The only way to learn about *Super Mario Bros.'* hidden shortcuts, warp zones, and glitches was through **word of mouth**. It happened at lunch tables, on the school bus, and in whispered conversations on the playground:

"If you duck at the end of World 1-2 and jump up the ceiling, you can skip to World 4."
"My cousin's friend said there's a secret World -1 that loops forever."
"If you jump over the flagpole, you can get to a hidden level."

Some of these turned out to be true (*yes, the Warp Zone exists*). Others were myths (*no, you can't get to a level beyond the flagpole*—except through weird glitches). But back then, **we didn't know what was real and what wasn't**. That was part of the magic.

We traded rumors like they were top-secret intel. And when someone *actually* pulled off one of the tricks—**when you saw a kid successfully warp to World 4 for the first time**—it felt like witnessing history.

The Urban Legends of *Super Mario Bros.*

Beyond the real secrets, *Super Mario Bros.* had **urban legends** that fascinated us. Some were just wishful thinking; others were the result of playground telephone, where a story got wilder every time it was retold.

- **The Minus World** – This one was real. If you performed a specific trick in World 1-2, you could reach a **glitched underwater level** that looped infinitely. Kids swore it led to another secret world, but really, it was just a programming error.
- **The Hidden Warp to World 9** – A total myth. Someone always claimed they "knew a guy" who found a hidden Warp Zone that went beyond World 8.
- **Finding Luigi in Single Player Mode** – Sorry, but Luigi was only available in two-player mode. That didn't stop kids from insisting there was a way to unlock him.
- **Jumping Over the Flagpole** – This one was partially true. In certain levels, you could actually glitch past the flagpole, but instead of reaching a secret world, you'd be stuck in an endless void.

These myths kept us talking for years. And since we *couldn't* just check the internet, **the mystery never really died**.

My First Encounter with Mario: The Deli Arcade Machine

Before *Super Mario Bros.* took over my living room, I first met Mario in the most sacred of childhood locations: **the corner deli up the street.**

Four blocks away, past the houses of kids I barely knew but nodded to anyway, sat a tiny deli with a couple of arcade machines crammed into the corner. One of them was **Mario Bros.**, the arcade game where Mario and Luigi cleared enemies out of pipes. I had never seen anything like it. The moment I heard that **coin-drop sound effect**, I was hooked.

I remember **digging into my pockets for every quarter I could find**—change from buying milk, spare coins from couch cushions, anything. I'd beg my parents for quarters like they were the most valuable thing on Earth. Because they *were*.

I wasn't great at the game, but that didn't matter. Every time I managed to clear a stage, I felt like a champion. Every lost life was a **lesson learned**, and every quarter spent was **an investment in skill**.

But nothing compared to **the Christmas I got my first Nintendo**.

The Christmas That Changed Everything

It was **the ultimate Christmas gift**—a brand-new **Nintendo Entertainment System**, complete with *Super Mario Bros.*. The moment I unwrapped it, I felt like I had just unlocked a new level of life itself.

Word spread **fast**. By that afternoon, kids from the neighborhood were **knocking on my door**, all wanting to see *Super Mario Bros.* in action. Some had played before; others were seeing it for the first time. It didn't matter—we all sat in the living room, **passing the controller, cheering each other on, and watching in awe as we tried to beat each level.**

And then, just as I thought I was getting good at the game, **my sister picked up the controller.**

The Frustration of Being Player 2 (And Watching My Sister Win)

Like most NES games, *Super Mario Bros.* was a **pass-the-controller** experience. In two-player mode, **Player 1 was Mario, Player 2 was Luigi**—but only one person played at a time. If you died, the other player took over.

And let me tell you… **being Player 2 was infuriating.**

- You didn't get to start first. You had to **sit there and watch** while Player 1 got all the action.
- If Player 1 was *really good*, you'd be waiting **forever** to play.
- When it was finally your turn, **you had all the pressure**—because if you messed up, you had to wait **all over again**.

And then there was **my sister**.

She had never played Mario before. But when she finally got her hands on the controller, she did something **unthinkable**—she **outplayed all of us.**

- She **didn't miss jumps**.
- She **figured out the Warp Zones faster than we did**.
- She **beat Bowser while we were still struggling with World 3**.

I couldn't believe it. Here I was, *the* gamer of the family, the one who spent **quarters at the deli machine**, and my sister—who had barely touched a controller—was **destroying all of us**.

She wasn't even smug about it. She just **shrugged and kept playing**, casually cruising through the game while the rest of us sat there in disbelief.

It was humbling. It was frustrating. But it was also **awesome**. Because that's what *Super Mario Bros.* was—it was **for everyone**.

Why *Super Mario Bros.* Still Matters

Nearly four decades later, *Super Mario Bros.* still **holds up**.

- The **controls are tight**, making Mario's jumps feel just right.
- The **level design is perfect**, introducing mechanics naturally without tutorials.
- The **secrets are still fun to find**, even if we now know them all.
- And the **nostalgia factor? Off the charts.**

For many of us, *Super Mario Bros.* **wasn't just a game**—it was an introduction to **a lifelong love of video games**. It was the reason we stayed up late on school nights, the cause of countless sibling rivalries, and the foundation for everything that came after.

Whether you played it in an arcade, on a friend's NES, or on Christmas morning in your own living room, **Mario was always there**—waiting for the next kid to pick up the controller and take on Bowser one more time.

Because some games never stop being fun. And *Super Mario Bros.*? It's one of the greatest of all time.

The Legend of Zelda – A World of Endless Wonder and Secrets

When *The Legend of Zelda* first arrived in 1986, it felt like **pure magic**. It wasn't just another video game—it was **an entire world**, filled with secrets, danger, and adventure. It wasn't a straight path from one level to the next; it was **open-ended**, mysterious, and seemingly *infinite*.

For a kid in the '80s, playing *The Legend of Zelda* was unlike anything else. It wasn't about just running to the right, like *Super Mario Bros.* Instead, **you could go anywhere.** Every direction led to something new—**a cave, a forest, a hidden dungeon, or a dead-end that just made you wonder if you were missing something.**

I never actually *beat The Legend of Zelda*—not because I didn't love it, but because **the world itself was the adventure**. Winning didn't feel as important as exploring. And every time I picked up the controller, I felt like there was something new to discover.

A World That Felt Infinite

Most NES games were **linear**—you moved from left to right, level by level, until you reached the end. But *The Legend of Zelda*? **It didn't tell you where to go.**

The moment you stepped into Hyrule, you were **on your own.**

- No arrows pointing you in the right direction.
- No tutorial explaining what to do.
- No one holding your hand.

You started with **nothing**—just an empty inventory and **a single cave** in front of you. If you didn't enter that cave, you could wander for hours, completely clueless about what to do. But if you did, you'd meet the mysterious old man who delivered **one of the most famous lines in gaming history**:

> *"It's dangerous to go alone! Take this."*

With that, you had your first sword. And from there, **the world was yours to explore.**

Hyrule seemed **massive**. The screen would scroll in all directions, leading to forests, graveyards, lakes, mountains, and endless mazes of enemies. And the best part? **It felt like there were secrets *everywhere*.**

The Magic of Secrets and Discovery

Unlike most games where secrets were rare, *The Legend of Zelda* **was built on secrets**.

- **Burn a bush?** Maybe there's a hidden staircase underneath.
- **Bomb a random rock?** It could reveal a cave full of rupees.
- **Push a tombstone?** You might find an underground passage.
- **Play the flute?** Something magical could happen.

Every square on the map had the *potential* to hide something. And since there was **no way to know for sure**, you just had to **experiment**.

Of course, as a kid, I didn't have a strategy guide or a map. The only way to figure things out was **trial and error—or word of mouth**. Sometimes I'd hear a friend at school say, *"Hey, if you bomb this specific rock, you'll find a secret dungeon."* Other times, I'd waste all my bombs on random walls, hoping for something that wasn't there.

But even when I *failed*, it didn't matter. The **thrill of discovering a new secret** was reward enough.

The Sound of the Flute: A Haunting, Magical Tune

One of my absolute favorite parts of *The Legend of Zelda* was the **flute.**

Music in NES games was usually simple, but Zelda's soundtrack was **different**—it felt **epic**, mysterious, and grand. And the flute? That was **something else entirely**.

When you played it, the screen would shake, the music would echo, and suddenly—**something would happen.**

- Sometimes, it would **warp you to another part of the map**, making you feel like you had unlocked some ancient, mystical power.
- Other times, it would **drain a lake**, revealing a hidden staircase.
- And sometimes… *nothing would happen at all*—leaving you to wonder if you just hadn't found the right place to play it yet.

The flute felt like **a key to an unseen world**—a tool that held *even more* secrets, waiting to be uncovered.

And that's what made Zelda so special: **the feeling that there was *always* something more to find.**

Never Beating the Game, But Never Needing To

I never beat *The Legend of Zelda*. Not because I didn't want to, but because **I never really felt the need to.**

Sure, I made progress. I found dungeons, defeated bosses, and collected pieces of the Triforce. But the goal never felt like **the most important part of the game**.

What mattered was **the journey itself**.

It was about:

- **Wandering into the graveyard**, feeling the eerie tension of ghostly enemies and wondering what secrets lay beneath the tombstones.
- **Stumbling upon a dungeon by accident**, entering a dark room with no idea what was waiting inside.
- **Fighting my way through lost woods**, convinced there had to be something *important* hidden beyond the trees.

And honestly? **The mystery was what made the game feel alive.**

Even years later, I still think about that *scrolling landscape of endless secrets*. The feeling that **the world of Hyrule was bigger than I'd ever fully understand**.

Why *The Legend of Zelda* Still Feels Magical Today

Even with modern games boasting massive open worlds, **nothing quite captures the magic of the original *Legend of Zelda***.

- It **trusted players** to figure things out on their own.
- It rewarded **curiosity and creativity** instead of just following a straight path.
- It made **every discovery feel personal**—because you *earned* it.
- It **felt bigger than it really was**, because the mystery was never fully solved.

Some games give you **a checklist**—Zelda gave you **a world**.

And even though I never reached the final boss, even though I never officially "won," I never felt like I *lost*. Because every time I turned on the game, there was **always something new waiting to be discovered**.

Even today, I still hear that **flute music** in my head and wonder…

What if I just played one more time? Maybe this time, I'd finally find all the secrets.

Tetris – The Game That Never Ends (Until It Does)

There are few games as timeless as *Tetris*. It doesn't have a story, it doesn't have characters, and it doesn't need them. It's just **falling blocks and an empty grid**—a simple idea that somehow became **one of the most addictive and iconic games of all time.**

But while *Tetris* was a hit in arcades and on early computers, **it wasn't until I played it on a Game Boy that I truly understood its magic.**

The First Time I Played *Tetris* on a Game Boy

I still remember **the first time I saw a Game Boy**. It wasn't mine—some other kid had one, and I was completely mesmerized. A **video game system that you could hold in your hands**? It felt like science fiction. And then I saw *Tetris* running on it—the blocks falling, the *do-do-do-do-do-do* music playing—and I knew I *had* to play it.

When I finally got my own Game Boy, *Tetris* was the **first game I played**. And from the moment I saw that monochrome screen light up, I was hooked.

- The **satisfying snap** of a piece locking into place.
- The **thrill of setting up a Tetris (clearing four lines at once).**
- The **panic of watching the stack get too high**, knowing you were about to lose.

Unlike other games where you had levels or bosses, *Tetris* was **pure endurance**. It wasn't about "beating" the game—it was about seeing how far you could go before **the inevitable.**

There was **no winning**—only **surviving**.

And yet, that's exactly what made it so addicting.

The Magic of Tetris on the Go

Before the Game Boy, video games were **tied to a TV**. You had to **be at home, plugged into a console** to play. But with *Tetris* on a Game Boy?

You could play **anywhere**.

- On long car rides, while staring out the window, hypnotized by falling blocks.
- At school, hiding behind a desk, trying to sneak in one more game.
- At night, under the covers, playing until your eyes couldn't stay open anymore.

It was the first time a game had **no limits**—no need for a TV, no need for a power outlet. Just **pop in the cartridge, turn it on, and start playing.**

And the best part? **That music.**

- **Type A:** The *classic*, fast-paced Russian folk-inspired theme that made every move feel more urgent.
- **Type B:** The *dramatic* tune that made it feel like you were solving a puzzle for the fate of humanity.
- **Type C:** The *calm*, almost lullaby-like music that made losing feel a little less painful.

Even now, decades later, I still hear that *Tetris* theme in my head.

From Survival to Mastery – How *Tetris* Changed Over the Years

Back in the Game Boy days, *Tetris* was a game of **seeing how long you could last**. You played **until the speed became impossible** or your mistakes piled up too high. There was **no ending**, only **failure**.

But then, something changed.

Over time, people **got better.**

- What used to be a game of endurance **became a game of precision**.
- What felt **impossible**—surviving at Level 20, pulling off constant Tetrises—became **normal** for top players.
- What seemed like an **endless challenge** suddenly had **a goal**: beating the game.

Yes, You Can Actually Beat *Tetris*

For years, *Tetris* was thought to be **unbeatable**—the game speeds up endlessly until human reflexes can't keep up.

But then, people started **figuring it out**.

- Players **learned advanced techniques**, like hypertapping and rolling, to move pieces faster than the game seemed to allow.
- They **memorized piece patterns**, recognizing placements in fractions of a second.
- They **pushed the limits of the human brain**, turning what was once chaos into **perfectly executed strategies**.

And then it happened.

In 2024, **the first person ever "beat"** *Tetris* on an NES by **crashing the game**. He got so far that the game literally **ran out of memory** and froze.

What once seemed **impossible** was now **achievable**.

And now? **It's happening regularly.**

A new generation of players, some who weren't even alive when the Game Boy came out, are **mastering *Tetris* in ways we never imagined.**

Why *Tetris* Still Matters

Even after all these years, *Tetris* is still **one of the greatest games ever made**.

- It **never gets old**—no matter how many times you play, there's *always* a new high score to chase.
- It's **easy to learn, but hard to master**—anyone can play, but only the best can truly dominate.
- It **trains your brain**—puzzle-solving, reflexes, pattern recognition, all in one.
- It's **everywhere**—from the original Game Boy to modern esports competitions.

And for me, *Tetris* will always be **the game that made handheld gaming feel like magic.**

I still remember that **first time** I held a Game Boy in my hands, saw those blocks fall, and felt the rush of clearing my first Tetris. I didn't know then that *Tetris* would still be around decades later, that people would eventually "beat" the unbeatable, that the game would evolve from **a simple puzzle** to **a global phenomenon.**

All I knew was that **I couldn't stop playing.**

And honestly? I still can't.

Street Fighter II – The Game That Turned Us into Warriors

Before *Street Fighter II*, video games were mostly about **beating the computer**—figuring out patterns, defeating AI enemies, and making it to the end. But when *Street Fighter II* hit arcades and home consoles, everything changed.

This wasn't just about **winning against the game**—this was about **proving yourself against other players**.

For the first time, a fighting game wasn't just about mashing buttons and hoping for the best. **Skill mattered.** Memorizing special moves, knowing when to strike, predicting your opponent's next move—these things **determined who walked away victorious**.

And if you were good? Oh, man. Nothing felt better than **landing a perfect combo** on an unsuspecting opponent and watching them crumble.

The Art of Memorizing Moves and Executing the Perfect Combo

One of the best parts of *Street Fighter II* was **learning the secret techniques of each fighter**. This wasn't just a game where you could button-mash your way to victory. **You had to practice.**

- You had to **master the quarter-circle forward motion** to throw a Hadouken.
- You had to **nail the timing** on charge moves like Guile's Sonic Boom.
- You had to **memorize attack combos**, so you could chain together devastating moves before your opponent even had a chance to react.

And when it all clicked—when you pulled off a **perfectly timed counterattack, dodged a fireball, and unleashed a crushing combo—it was the best feeling in the world.**

Playing as Blanka – The Wild Card of *Street Fighter II*

For me, **Blanka was the ultimate fighter.** He wasn't just strong—he was *chaotic*.

- His **Electric Thunder attack** let him sit there and *zap* anyone foolish enough to get too close.
- His **Rolling Attack** let him launch across the screen **like a missile**, catching opponents off guard.
- His **wild, animal-like fighting style** made him unpredictable.

Blanka wasn't just about brute force—he was about **throwing your opponent off their game**.

There was nothing better than **baiting someone into attacking, only to zap them with an electric shock**. Or launching across the screen and watching them **desperately try to block** as I landed hit after hit.

Blanka wasn't the most traditional fighter, but that's what made him **so much fun to play.**

The Multiplayer Legends – Kings of the Arcade

Every arcade had *that one player*—the **local legend**. The one who could **destroy anyone who stepped up to challenge them.**

These guys didn't just play *Street Fighter II*—they **lived** it.

- They **knew every character's move set by heart**.
- They **could predict your next move** before you even pressed the button.
- They **never lost—and if they did, they always came back stronger.**

Watching a true master play *Street Fighter II* was like **watching an artist at work**. They weren't just button-mashing—they were **strategizing, reacting, and controlling the entire match** with their movements.

These were the guys who knew exactly **how to counter every attack, how to pull off insane combos, and how to make you feel completely helpless**. And if you were lucky enough to **beat one of them**, it was **a moment you'd never forget.**

The Birth of a Massive Fighting Game Community

Street Fighter II didn't just create a **game**—it created a **community**.

- **Tournaments** started popping up, with the best players from all over battling for supremacy.
- **Other fighting games** started following its lead—*Mortal Kombat*, *Tekken*, *King of Fighters*, and countless others.
- **The fighting game scene exploded**, and it never stopped growing.

Even today, decades later, *Street Fighter* is still **one of the most respected fighting games in the world**. The **Evolution Championship Series (EVO)**, the biggest fighting game tournament on the planet, is packed with players competing in *Street Fighter*, showing off **insane levels of skill that most of us can only dream of.**

Why *Street Fighter II* Still Reigns Supreme

Even with all the fighting games that have come after it, ***Street Fighter II* is still a legend**.

- It was **the first game to make fighting games competitive**—a battle of skill, reflexes, and strategy.
- It had **tight, balanced gameplay** that made matches exciting and unpredictable.
- It gave players **a reason to practice, master characters, and prove themselves.**

And for those of us who grew up **memorizing combos, shocking our friends with Blanka, and trying to take down the best player at the arcade**, *Street Fighter II* will **always** hold a special place in gaming history.

Because in the end, **nothing beats the feeling of victory when you outthink, outplay, and outfight your opponent.**

Sonic the Hedgehog – The Blue Blur That Changed Gaming Forever

The year I got my **Sega Genesis** for Christmas was **one of the greatest moments of my childhood**. Up until then, I had been a Nintendo kid—Mario was the king, and platformers had a certain, steady rhythm to them. But when I unwrapped that black box with its sleek, futuristic design, **I had no idea my entire view of gaming was about to change.**

That Christmas morning, I didn't just get one game—I got **two**: *Sonic the Hedgehog* and *Joe Montana Sports Talk Football*. One game let me tear through levels **faster than anything I had ever seen before**, while the other made me feel like I was actually playing **real** football with its incredible play-by-play commentary.

But as much fun as *Joe Montana Sports Talk Football* was, it was **Sonic that stole the show.**

The Moment I First Played *Sonic the Hedgehog*

From the moment I powered on the Genesis and saw that **Sega logo flash across the screen** (with that unforgettable "SEGA!" chime), I knew I was in for something different.

And then, **Sonic appeared**—tapping his foot, arms crossed, looking impatient, like he was waiting for me to catch up. **This wasn't Mario.** This was a character with attitude, a speed demon ready to take off.

And when I pressed start, **everything changed.**

Green Hill Zone loaded up, and before I even had time to process the vibrant, **beautifully detailed world**, Sonic **took off like a rocket.**

- The speed was **unbelievable**—far beyond anything I had played before.
- The world wasn't just a series of blocks—it was **loop-de-loops, corkscrews, and huge hills to roll down** at breakneck speeds.
- The **music**—that infectious, upbeat Green Hill Zone theme—made it feel like I was **on the adventure of a lifetime.**

The **first time I hit a ramp and launched into the air, flipping as I flew across the screen,** I knew this wasn't just another platformer. **This was something special.**

The Sound of Rings – The Most Satisfying Noise in Gaming

One of the greatest things about *Sonic the Hedgehog* wasn't just the speed—it was the **sound**.

The **ring collection sound effect** was **pure magic**. There was something **deeply satisfying** about flying through the air, rolling into a row of golden rings, and hearing that **shimmering chime** as Sonic scooped them up.

It was the kind of sound that made you **want more**—you weren't just playing to beat the level; you were playing to **collect every single ring you could find**. And that meant **exploring every part of the stage, launching off ramps, and racing through hidden paths to grab them all.**

But the moment you got hit by an enemy?

Absolute heartbreak.

The instant **chaos** of Sonic losing all his rings—watching them scatter across the screen, frantically trying to grab at least one before they all disappeared—it was the ultimate **highs and lows of gaming**.

Sonic Was More Than Just Speed – It Was Exploration

One of the most brilliant things about *Sonic the Hedgehog* was that it wasn't just about **going fast**—it was about **figuring out how to use that speed wisely.**

- Some paths were **high up**, requiring careful platforming and momentum-based jumps.
- Other paths were **down low**, where you could blaze through obstacles at max speed, but at the risk of missing secrets.
- If you **stayed alert**, you could find secret paths, hidden rings, and shortcuts that let you speed through a level faster than you ever thought possible.

There was **a skill** to Sonic—knowing **when to go full speed and when to slow down** and explore.

Christmas Day: The Genesis Took Over the Living Room

That Christmas, my Sega Genesis wasn't just **my** gift—it became **the centerpiece of the living room.**

- Family members stopped to watch as I zipped through loops, amazed at how **fast and smooth** the game looked.

- My friends **came over to play**, each one taking turns, trying to **go faster, collect more rings, and reach further into the game.**
- Even my parents—who never cared about video games—were **impressed by how different Sonic felt from anything they had seen before.**

That entire Christmas break was **pure gaming bliss.** I spent hours **learning every stage,** figuring out **where all the hidden extra lives were,** and trying to master **that perfect balance of speed and control.**

And every time I booted up *Sonic the Hedgehog,* that **opening chime of the SEGA logo** felt like a welcome back to **the fastest, coolest adventure I had ever played.**

Why *Sonic the Hedgehog* Was a Game-Changer

Looking back, *Sonic the Hedgehog* wasn't just an **awesome game**—it was **a revolution.**

- **It introduced true speed to platformers** – No other game moved like *Sonic.* It **felt futuristic** compared to Mario's slower, more methodical pace.
- **It made exploration exciting** – Instead of one clear path, each level had **multiple routes,** rewarding players who experimented.
- **It had attitude** – Sonic **wasn't just another silent hero.** He tapped his foot if you stood still, **rolled his eyes if you took too long,** and had the energy of a character who wasn't just *saving the world*—he was **having fun doing it.**
- **The sound design was iconic** – The ring collection, the spring launch sound, the satisfying *boing* of bouncing off an enemy—it all made the game feel **alive.**

And perhaps most importantly?

Sonic **became the face of Sega.** He wasn't just a character—he was a **symbol of an entirely new gaming experience.** If Mario was the friendly, reliable plumber, **Sonic was the rebellious, cool speedster** who **turned video games into a thrill ride.**

The Legacy of That Christmas Morning

That Christmas when I got my Sega Genesis, I didn't just get a **game console**—I got **an entire new way of playing games.**

Joe Montana Sports Talk Football was **cool,** and I loved how it felt like **watching a real game with its running commentary.** But *Sonic the Hedgehog*? That was **something else entirely.** It was the game that **redefined what I thought was possible** in a video game.

Even today, when I hear the sound of **rings being collected,** or see Sonic rev up for a spin dash, I'm instantly transported back to **that Christmas morning**—sitting in front of the TV, controller in hand, **blasting through Green Hill Zone at lightning speed, grinning ear to ear.**

Because *Sonic the Hedgehog* wasn't just **a game I played**.

It was **a game that made me fall in love with gaming all over again.**

GoldenEye 007 – The Multiplayer King of the '90s

If you grew up in the late '90s and had an N64, chances are *GoldenEye 007* was a central part of your gaming experience. It was more than just a first-person shooter—it was *the* game that defined sleepovers, after-school gaming sessions, and neighborhood rivalries. While the single-player campaign was excellent, it was **the multiplayer mode that cemented GoldenEye's legendary status**.

No online play, no fancy voice chat—just **four players huddled around a single TV, fighting for bragging rights.** The multiplayer experience was pure, chaotic joy, often leading to intense rivalries, house rules, and some of the most legendary gaming moments of our childhood.

The Birth of the "Screen Cheating" Era

Unlike today's online shooters where players have their own screens, *GoldenEye* was **local split-screen multiplayer**—meaning every player could see what their opponents were doing. And this led to one of the most notorious, unspoken (but totally common) aspects of the game: **screen cheating**.

We all had that one friend—maybe even *you*—who always knew exactly where you were, no matter how well you hid. "*How did you find me so fast?!*" someone would yell, only to hear the inevitable reply:

"Dude, I wasn't looking at your screen, I just knew you were there."

Spoiler alert: He was totally looking at your screen.

This led to one of the most hilarious and creative modifications to living room battle arenas: **cardboard dividers taped to the TV.** Kids desperate to prevent screen cheating would go full DIY mode, cutting out pieces of cardboard or poster board and taping them across the middle of the screen. Some setups were so elaborate that players would literally crouch under or behind bedsheets hanging from the ceiling just to avoid giving away their position.

Of course, none of this *really* worked—everyone still cheated. But the effort alone showed just how intense these multiplayer matches could get.

The One Kid Who Was Unstoppable

Every friend group had **that one guy**. The *GoldenEye* prodigy. The one kid who **never lost**, no matter how hard you tried. He knew every map by heart, memorized the spawn locations for weapons, and could pull off headshots with the PP7 pistol like it was nothing.

- He was the guy who **always picked Oddjob**, the infamously short character who was borderline impossible to hit (and universally banned in most friend groups).
- He **controlled The Facility**, knowing exactly how to trap you in the bathroom and gun you down before you could even grab a weapon.
- He **knew all the secret locations** and had a sixth sense for where you'd be hiding.
- He could land **a one-shot kill with the Golden Gun** before you even had time to react.

And the worst part? He was always annoyingly casual about it.

"*Bro, you just gotta get good,*" he'd say after wrecking you for the 20th time in a row.

Some kids got so desperate to beat the *GoldenEye* master that **alliances were formed**—temporary truces where three kids would gang up against the reigning champ, only for the truce to fall apart in an inevitable betrayal as soon as one of them saw an opportunity for victory.

Epic Multiplayer Moments That Defined the Era

The beauty of *GoldenEye's* multiplayer wasn't just the competition—it was the sheer **chaos and hilarity** that unfolded in every match. Here are a few moments that every *GoldenEye* veteran can relate to:

The Facility Bathroom Massacre

If you spawned in *The Facility*, you knew the **bathroom was a death trap**. Some kid would always **camp the vents**, dropping down onto unsuspecting victims, while another lurked by the door waiting for fresh respawns. If you somehow survived long enough to get a weapon, the hallways became **a nightmare of proximity mines**—because every kid who got their hands on them immediately **booby-trapped the entire level**.

Slappers-Only Mode—The True Test of Friendship

For some reason, every friend group eventually tried **Slappers-Only Mode**—a setting where guns were disabled, forcing players to attack each other with slow, awkward karate chops. What started as a joke turned into **one of the most ridiculous and frustrating gaming experiences of all time**, as everyone ran around in circles desperately trying to land a slap.

The Rage-Inducing Remote Mines

Remote mines were the ultimate troll weapon. Every match had at least one kid who would **cover entire rooms with explosives**, then hide and wait for an unlucky opponent to walk in before **detonating them with maniacal laughter**. If you were really evil, you'd **stick a mine to an armor pickup**, ensuring the next desperate player who went for it would be instantly vaporized.

Playing License to Kill Mode and Realizing Just How Bad You Are

In normal mode, you could take a few hits before going down. But in **License to Kill Mode**, it was *one-shot kills*—which meant the guy with the fastest trigger finger *always* won. If you weren't that guy, well… let's just say you spent most of the match **respawning**.

That One Friend Who Wouldn't Stop Pausing the Game

There was *always* one person who would **pause the game mid-battle**—whether it was to change their control scheme, adjust the sensitivity, or just mess with everyone. This usually resulted in a *very real* punch to the arm from the other players.

Why *GoldenEye* Still Matters

Even though *GoldenEye* is over 25 years old, its impact on gaming is still felt today. It was one of the first console shooters to **nail multiplayer gameplay**, paving the way for games like *Halo*, *Call of Duty*, and *Battlefield*. But more than that, it was **a cultural phenomenon**—a game that brought friends together, created lifelong rivalries, and gave us some of the most unforgettable gaming moments of our childhood.

Sure, if you play it today, the controls feel clunky compared to modern shooters. But that doesn't matter. *GoldenEye* wasn't about mechanics—it was about **the experience**. The laughter, the arguments, the ridiculous tactics, and the friendships that were formed (and sometimes *broken*) along the way.

And let's be honest—if someone challenged you to a *GoldenEye* match today, you'd still pick up that N64 controller, dust off your old skills, and **try to reclaim your childhood glory**. Because once a *GoldenEye* player, always a *GoldenEye* player.

Final Fantasy – The Game That Changed Everything

There are games that are **great**, games that are **legendary**, and then there are games like *Final Fantasy* —titles that **completely redefine an entire genre** and leave a permanent mark on gaming history.

Before *Final Fantasy* came out, Japanese RPGs were **still somewhat niche in the West**. Sure, some gamers had played *Final Fantasy IV* and *VI* (released as *II* and *III* in North America), and franchises like *Dragon Quest* had a loyal following, but JRPGs weren't **mainstream** outside of Japan.

Then came *Final Fantasy*.

This wasn't just a game—it was **an experience**. A sweeping **epic filled with deep storytelling, unforgettable characters, and cinematic moments that left players in awe**. It was the kind of game that **people still talk about decades later**.

And in some cases, it's **the reason people still buy new consoles today.**

A Game That Defined a Generation

When *Final Fantasy VII* launched in 1997, it was **unlike anything we had seen before**.

- It had **3D character models** (a massive leap from the 2D sprites of past games).
- The world was **huge, sprawling, and visually stunning for its time**.
- The **cinematic cutscenes** were groundbreaking—at a time when most games had simple text-based storytelling, *FFVII* gave us **full-motion video sequences that made the game feel like an interactive movie.**

And the story? **It hit differently.**

This wasn't a **simple good-vs-evil tale**—it was filled with **political intrigue, deep emotional moments, and characters with complex backstories**.

- **Cloud Strife**, the ex-SOLDIER with a past full of mystery and trauma.
- **Sephiroth**, one of the most menacing and iconic villains in gaming history.
- **Aerith**, whose fate still haunts gamers to this day.

It wasn't just a game—it was **a journey.**

The Game That Kept Us Talking

One of the **most fascinating things about** *Final Fantasy VII* is how **it never really went away.**

Even today, I know friends who have been **playing the series since the very first game released in the '80s**, and for them, *Final Fantasy VII* is **still the one that stands above the rest**.

And then there's Joe.

Joe isn't the kind of gamer who **buys every console at launch or keeps up with all the latest releases**. But when a new *Final Fantasy* game comes out? That's **a different story**.

- He bought a **PlayStation 2** for *Final Fantasy X*.
- He bought a **PlayStation 3** for *Final Fantasy XIII*.
- And when the *Final Fantasy VII Remake* was announced? He didn't hesitate—**PlayStation 4, day one.**

For some gamers, *Final Fantasy VII* isn't just **a great RPG**—it's **the reason they still play games at all**.

The Influence of *Final Fantasy VII* on the RPG Genre

Even if you've never played *Final Fantasy VII*, you've **felt its impact**.

🎮 **JRPGs Became Mainstream in the West** – After *FFVII*, Japanese RPGs **exploded in popularity**, paving the way for games like *Persona*, *Xenogears*, and *Kingdom Hearts*.

🎮 **Cinematic Storytelling Became Standard** – Before *FFVII*, most RPGs had **text-heavy dialogue and static screens**. Now, every major RPG **uses cutscenes, voice acting, and cinematics to enhance storytelling**.

🎮 **Gaming's Emotional Potential Was Proven** – *FFVII* was one of the first games that made players **genuinely feel deep emotions for its characters**. It set the standard for **story-driven gaming experiences**.

Why *Final Fantasy VII* Still Matters Today

Even decades later, *Final Fantasy VII* remains **one of the most beloved games of all time**. It's been remastered, re-released, and even **rebuilt from the ground up** with the *Final Fantasy VII Remake*.

But for those of us who played it back in the day, it's not just about the **graphics, the turn-based combat, or even the story itself**.

It's about the **memories**.

It's about **staying up late grinding for Limit Breaks, finally defeating Emerald Weapon after dozens of failed attempts**, and **arguing with friends over which characters made the best party**.

It's about **Joe buying a whole console just to relive a piece of his childhood**.

It's about **a game that wasn't just played—it was lived.**

Metal Gear Solid – The Game That Made Us Feel Like Real Spies

In the late '90s, video games were still mostly about running, jumping, shooting, and collecting power-ups. Then along came *Metal Gear Solid*, a game that didn't just ask you to fight enemies—it **asked you to outthink them**.

Hideo Kojima's masterpiece wasn't just a game; it was an experience. It was **the first time many of us felt like we were truly inside a spy thriller**, sneaking through high-security compounds, hiding in cardboard boxes, and listening to gripping conversations that unfolded like a Hollywood blockbuster.

This wasn't a game where you could just run in guns blazing (though some of us *tried*). *Metal Gear Solid* demanded patience, strategy, and creativity. It gave us moments of sheer frustration, pure amazement, and some of the most unforgettable twists in gaming history.

Hiding in Boxes and Outsmarting Guards: The Thrill of Stealth Gaming

Before *Metal Gear Solid*, most games revolved around combat—you saw an enemy, you shot them. But this game introduced many of us to **stealth mechanics**, forcing us to think like a real secret agent.

Guards weren't just mindless drones—they **reacted** to what you did. If they heard footsteps, they'd investigate. If they saw footprints in the snow, they'd follow them. If they spotted you, they'd sound an alarm, and suddenly the entire base was hunting you down.

That meant you had to be creative.

- **Hiding in cardboard boxes** – It sounded ridiculous, but somehow, it *worked*. Crawling into a box and staying perfectly still as a guard walked past was both nerve-wracking and hilarious. And if the coast was clear, you'd just *shuffle* across the floor, box and all, hoping no one would notice.
- **Knocking on walls to distract enemies** – You could tap on a surface, and a guard would actually come over to investigate, leaving their post unguarded. This was mind-blowing at the time—video game enemies weren't supposed to be *this* smart!
- **Crawling through vents and sneaking past cameras** – It was like we were actually inside a spy movie. Every inch of progress felt like a personal victory, every enemy evaded felt like a stroke of genius.

The tension of sneaking through Shadow Moses Island was unmatched. Every time you heard that *alert sound*—that dreaded "!" over a guard's head—your heart would race. Could you escape before backup arrived? Could you find the perfect hiding spot before they searched the area?

No game had ever made us feel like this before.

The Frustration (and Genius) of Fighting Psycho Mantis

Then came one of *Metal Gear Solid's* most **mind-blowing moments**—the battle with **Psycho Mantis**.

At first, it felt like an **impossible** boss fight. Every time you moved, Psycho Mantis *already knew what you were going to do*. He dodged every punch, every bullet, every attack. He was **literally reading your mind**.

And just when frustration was setting in, he started **messing with your head in real life.**

- He **read your memory card**, commenting on your saved games (*"Oh… I see you like playing Castlevania."*).
- He **made your controller vibrate**, claiming he was using his psychic powers.
- He **turned the screen black** for a few seconds, making you think your TV had shut off.

At the time, this was **witchcraft**. No other game had **broken the fourth wall** like this.

But then, through trial and error (or maybe from a friend who figured it out first), you discovered the **insane, never-before-seen solution**:

You had to physically unplug your controller and plug it into the second controller port.

Suddenly, he couldn't read your moves anymore. His psychic powers were useless. And just like that, the fight became winnable.

This was pure **genius**. Hideo Kojima had just forced players to **think outside the game itself**—to manipulate the **physical hardware** in order to win. No one had ever done anything like this before.

The First Playthrough: A Cinematic Experience Unlike Any Other

Playing *Metal Gear Solid* for the first time wasn't just about sneaking around and taking down enemies—it was about being completely **immersed** in a story that felt bigger than anything we'd seen before in a video game.

It had everything:

- **Movie-quality cutscenes** – The opening sequence alone, with Snake sneaking into the base via an underwater infiltration, set the tone for something **far beyond a typical action game**.
- **Incredible voice acting** – Characters like Solid Snake, Liquid Snake, and Revolver Ocelot felt **real**. Their dialogue was gripping, intense, and filled with intrigue.
- **Plot twists and betrayals** – From the shocking reveal of who the real enemy was to the emotional gut punch of Sniper Wolf's fate, the story constantly surprised you.
- **A complex, fully fleshed-out world** – Shadow Moses wasn't just a backdrop; it felt like a **real place**, with security systems, hostage situations, and political conspiracies unfolding around you.

Even the **boss fights** were next level:

- **The sniper duel with Sniper Wolf** – One of the most intense, nerve-wracking battles ever, where you had to find cover, stay patient, and take the perfect shot.
- **The tank battle against Vulcan Raven** – Dodging cannon fire in an open field, sneaking between cover points—it felt like an action movie sequence come to life.
- **The final fistfight with Liquid Snake** – A brutal, cinematic showdown on top of a Metal Gear, where you settled everything with your bare fists.

And then, of course, came **the escape sequence**—a high-speed chase in a jeep, racing against time as the entire base collapsed around you. It was **pure adrenaline**, the perfect climax to an already unforgettable experience.

Why *Metal Gear Solid* Was a Game-Changer

Looking back, *Metal Gear Solid* wasn't just a great game—it was **revolutionary**. It took gaming into a new era, one where storytelling, immersion, and creativity were just as important as gameplay.

- It showed us that **stealth could be just as exciting as combat**.
- It broke the fourth wall in ways no game ever had before.
- It introduced **voice acting that actually felt like a movie**, setting a new standard for gaming narratives.
- It made us **feel** like spies—clever, resourceful, and always one step ahead (except when we weren't).

And even today, the magic of *Metal Gear Solid* is still there. Whether you're replaying it for nostalgia or experiencing it for the first time, the thrill of sneaking through Shadow Moses, outsmarting enemies, and *finally* beating Psycho Mantis is just as incredible as it was in 1998.

Because some games are **timeless**. And *Metal Gear Solid*? It's one of the greatest of all time.

Why These Games Still Hold Up Today

Many classic games still feel fresh because they focused on **gameplay first**. Unlike modern games that sometimes rely on massive updates, microtransactions, or open-ended grinds, older games had:

- **Tight mechanics** – Everything felt precise, from *Mario's* jump to *Street Fighter's* combos.
- **Instant accessibility** – No long tutorials; just pick up and play.
- **Challenging but fair difficulty** – You learned through playing, not from constant hints or checkpoints.
- **Memorable soundtracks** – The music from games like *Mega Man 2*, *Castlevania*, and *Chrono Trigger* is still legendary today.

Thanks to re-releases, remasters, and emulation, many of these games are **easier than ever to play today**—whether through official collections (*The Cowabunga Collection* for TMNT fans, *Sega Genesis Classics* for retro Sega games) or fan-made restorations.

Hidden Gems You Might Have Missed

Not every classic game was a mainstream hit. Some were overlooked but are absolute must-plays for any retro gamer today.

ActRaiser – SNES

A strange but brilliant mix of side-scrolling action and city-building, *ActRaiser* is a game that defied genre expectations. You played as a god-like being who fought demons but also had to rebuild civilizations—something completely unique at the time.

Zombies Ate My Neighbors – SNES/Genesis

This quirky co-op action game was *pure fun*, with horror-movie-inspired levels, creative weapons (squirt guns, anyone?), and a wacky sense of humor. It's still a blast to play today.

Comix Zone – Sega Genesis

An underrated beat 'em up where you played as a comic book artist trapped in his own creation. The game's visual style—literally playing through a comic book—was ahead of its time.

The Guardian Legend – NES

A mix of top-down shooting and Zelda-style exploration, this game never got the love it deserved. If you enjoy sci-fi and challenging gameplay, it's worth checking out.

Final Thoughts

The games of the '80s and '90s weren't just "good for their time"—they're still some of the best-designed games ever made. Whether you're revisiting them for nostalgia or experiencing them for the first time, they prove that great gameplay never gets old.

In the next chapter, we'll explore **how to build the ultimate retro gaming setup**—whether you want to collect original hardware, use emulation, or find the best ways to play these classics in the modern age.

Chapter 2: Building a Retro Gaming Setup in 2025

There's something magical about **playing the games you grew up with**—not just remembering them, but actually sitting down with a controller, hearing that familiar start-up chime, and diving back into the classics.

But if you've tried hooking up an NES, SNES, Sega Genesis, or PlayStation 1 to a modern TV, you know it's not always that simple. The way we experience games has changed dramatically, and while retro gaming is more popular than ever, finding **the best way to play old-school games today** comes with some choices.

Do you hunt down **original hardware** for an authentic experience? Do you embrace **emulation** for convenience? Or do you opt for **modern mini consoles** that bring the classics to life with plug-and-play simplicity?

This chapter will break down the best ways to build a **retro gaming setup in 2025**, no matter what kind of experience you're looking for.

Playing Retro Games on a Modern TV

One of the biggest challenges in retro gaming is **compatibility with modern TVs**.

- Older consoles were designed for **CRT televisions**, using **composite (red, white, yellow) cables** or **RF adapters**.
- Modern TVs rely on **HDMI** and have **input lag** that can make older games feel sluggish.
- Some classic consoles don't even display correctly on new TVs—resulting in **blurry, stretched, or laggy visuals**.

The Solutions:

1. **HD Retro Converters & Upscalers** – Devices like the **Retrotink 5X** or **Open Source Scan Converter (OSSC)** take old-school video signals and **convert them to crisp, lag-free HDMI**. These are **pricey but incredible** if you want **the most authentic experience** on a modern display.
2. **Emulation & FPGA Consoles** – Modern devices like the **Analogue Pocket (for Game Boy games)** or the **MiSTer FPGA (for multiple classic systems) recreate** old consoles **without** the need for original hardware.
3. **Mini Consoles & Remakes** – Systems like the **SNES Classic, Sega Genesis Mini, and PlayStation Classic** provide a **plug-and-play** experience with **HDMI support right out of the box**.

4. **Retro-Friendly TVs** – Some hardcore enthusiasts **seek out CRTs**, but if space is an issue, **certain gaming monitors** and TVs with **low input lag and good scaling** (like some LG OLEDs) work great.

Original Hardware vs. Emulation vs. Mini Consoles

Each method of playing retro games has its advantages and disadvantages.

Option 1: Original Hardware (For the Purists)

There's nothing quite like **playing on the original console with the original controllers**. The weight of the controller, the feel of the buttons, even the slight quirks of each system **bring back memories in a way that nothing else can**.

■ **Pros:**

- **The most authentic experience**—everything feels exactly how it did back in the day.
- **No compatibility issues with cartridges or discs** (as long as they work).
- **A collector's dream**—owning physical consoles, cartridges, and accessories feels special.

✕ Cons:

- **Aging hardware**—consoles and controllers wear out, disc drives fail, and capacitors degrade.
- **Difficult to connect to modern TVs**—requires extra adapters or CRTs.
- **Expensive**—rare games and accessories can cost a **fortune**.

Option 2: Emulation (For Convenience & Customization)

If you want to **play everything on one device**, emulation is the way to go. From **RetroArch** to **Raspberry Pi builds** to high-end FPGA-based systems like **MiSTer**, emulation allows you to play **hundreds of classic games without needing physical cartridges**.

■ **Pros:**

- **Huge library**—play thousands of games from different systems on one device.
- **Save states & mods**—rewind mistakes, save anywhere, and tweak graphics.
- **Portable**—play on a PC, Steam Deck, or even a phone.

✕ Cons:

- **Not always perfect**—some emulators don't match original hardware exactly.

- **Legal gray area**—while emulation itself is legal, **downloading ROMs of games you don't own isn't**.
- **Lack of nostalgia factor**—playing an N64 game on a keyboard just doesn't feel the same.

Option 3: Mini Consoles (For Plug-and-Play Simplicity)

Over the past few years, companies have released **mini versions of classic consoles**, including the **NES Classic, SNES Classic, Sega Genesis Mini, and PlayStation Classic**. These systems come preloaded with a selection of games and **connect directly to modern TVs via HDMI**.

■ **Pros:**

- **Super easy to use**—plug it in and start playing.
- **No need to track down old cartridges or discs**.
- **Affordable**—cheaper than buying original hardware or high-end emulation setups.

✕ **Cons:**

- **Limited game selection**—you can't just pop in a cartridge.
- **Some mini consoles are better than others**—the PlayStation Classic, for example, had poor emulation at launch.
- **Not quite the same as the real thing**—though they look and feel close, some hardcore fans prefer original hardware.

The Ultimate Retro Gaming Accessories

To **enhance your retro gaming setup**, a few key accessories can **make a big difference** in your experience.

1. Wireless Retro Controllers

While wired controllers offer **that classic feel**, wireless options like **8BitDo's SNES and Genesis-style controllers** provide the **same nostalgic design without the clutter**.

2. Flash Carts & Optical Drive Emulators

If you **own original hardware** but don't want to spend **hundreds of dollars on rare cartridges**, devices like the **EverDrive (for NES, SNES, Genesis, etc.)** let you **play multiple games from one cartridge**. For disc-based systems like PlayStation and Sega Saturn, Optical Drive Emulators (ODEs) let you **play games from an SD card, bypassing aging disc drives**.

3. Retro CRT Filters & Scanline Shaders

For **those using modern TVs**, enabling **scanline filters** or **shaders** can help mimic the look of a CRT screen, adding **softness and pixel blending** that make classic games look better than a **raw pixel-perfect display**.

4. Custom Arcade Sticks & Fight Pads

For arcade and fighting game fans, investing in a **quality arcade stick** (like a Hori or Mad Catz model) **transforms the experience**, making it feel closer to **playing on an actual arcade machine**.

Building the Retro Gaming Setup That's Right for You

At the end of the day, **there's no single "best" way to play retro games**—it all comes down to what matters most to you.

- **If you want authenticity?** Get original hardware and a good scaler for modern TVs.
- **If you want convenience?** Go with a mini console or an FPGA-based system.
- **If you want a massive library?** Emulation is the way to go.

No matter which route you take, **retro gaming in 2025 is better than ever**. Whether you're firing up an NES on a CRT, playing Sonic on a Genesis Mini, or revisiting *Street Fighter II* on a custom arcade stick, **one thing remains true**:

These games **never get old**—and thanks to modern technology, they'll be around for generations to come.

Chapter 3: Collecting and Restoring Classic Games

For many gamers, playing retro games isn't just about nostalgia—it's about **preserving a piece of gaming history**. Whether it's tracking down your childhood favorites, uncovering rare gems, or restoring classic consoles to their former glory, **collecting and maintaining retro games** has become a passionate hobby for many.

But if you've ever searched for classic games, you know **prices can be insane**. Finding a decent-condition **NES, SNES, or Sega Genesis game at a fair price** is tougher than ever, and some titles sell for hundreds (or even thousands) of dollars. Add in the fact that old consoles and discs **deteriorate over time**, and retro collecting quickly becomes both **a challenge and an adventure**.

This chapter will guide you through **where to find classic games without breaking the bank, how to restore and maintain your collection, and how to build the ultimate retro gaming room.**

Finding Classic Games Without Overpaying

Back in the day, you could find **cheap retro games** at yard sales, flea markets, and used game stores. Now, thanks to **the rise of retro gaming and online resellers**, prices have skyrocketed. But if you know where to look, you can **still find great deals.**

Best Places to Find Classic Games

■ Local Thrift Stores & Flea Markets

- Many people **don't realize the value of old video games**, so **thrift stores and flea markets** can still be goldmines.
- Be prepared to **dig through random bins**—sometimes the best finds are buried.
- Always **check for hidden treasures** behind the counter—many stores keep games separate from their usual stock.

■ Garage Sales & Estate Sales

- Many people **sell off old gaming collections without knowing their worth.**
- **Early morning shoppers get the best deals**—so arrive before the crowds.
- **Bundle deals can be your best friend**—buying a console **with** a stack of games is often cheaper than buying individual titles.

■ Local Retro Game Stores

- While not always the cheapest, **small independent game shops** often have **fair prices, knowledgeable staff, and trade-in deals**.
- Many stores **clean and test their games**, so you're less likely to buy a dud.
- Some shops **let you test a game before you buy it**, ensuring it works properly.

■ Online Marketplaces (eBay, Facebook Marketplace, OfferUp, Craigslist)

- **eBay is a great place for rare finds**, but watch out for **overpriced listings and fakes**.
- **Facebook Marketplace, OfferUp, and Craigslist** often have **local sellers with better deals**—you just have to be fast before someone else grabs them.
- Always **check for scratches, missing manuals, and counterfeit cartridges** before buying.

■ Retro Gaming Conventions

- **Gaming expos and conventions** often have **huge selections** of retro games at competitive prices.
- Some sellers are willing to **haggle**, especially toward the end of an event.
- It's also a great place to **meet other collectors and learn about the market**.

◼ **Japanese Import Sites (For Hidden Gems & Cheaper Prices)**

- Many retro games were **cheaper in Japan**, and if you don't mind playing in Japanese (or using a translation patch), importing can save you **a ton of money**.
- Sites like **Yahoo Auctions Japan, Surugaya, and Mandarake** offer **authentic retro games at lower prices** than Western markets.

Restoring and Maintaining Classic Games & Consoles

Finding a rare game is one thing—**keeping it in good condition is another**. Over time, cartridges, discs, and consoles **degrade**, but with proper care, they can last for **decades**.

Cleaning & Restoring Cartridges

☐ **For NES, SNES, Genesis & Other Cartridge-Based Games:**

- **Clean the contacts** – Use **91% isopropyl alcohol and a cotton swab** to clean the metal connectors.
- **Remove corrosion** – A **pink pencil eraser** can scrub off mild corrosion on the contacts.
- **Avoid blowing into cartridges** – It was common back in the day, but your breath introduces **moisture**, which can lead to corrosion over time.

☐ **For Game Boy, N64, and Other Handheld Cartridges:**

- Use the same **alcohol cleaning method** as NES games.
- Store cartridges **vertically** to avoid dust buildup inside the pins.

Cleaning & Restoring Disc-Based Games

☐ **For PlayStation 1, Dreamcast, and Other Disc-Based Games:**

- **Light scratches?** Use a **soft microfiber cloth** to clean the disc from the center outward.
- **Deep scratches?** A game resurfacing machine like the **JFJ Easy Pro** can help remove deeper scratches.
- **Do NOT use toothpaste** – This old myth **can actually damage the disc further**.

For Consoles with Disc Drives:

- **Laser lenses wear out over time**—if your system **struggles to read discs**, use a **disc lens cleaner** or replace the laser.
- **PS2, Xbox, and GameCube disc drives** can sometimes be **adjusted manually** to improve reading performance.

Keeping Consoles in Working Condition

1 Capacitor Replacements

- Many older consoles (especially **Sega CD, TurboGrafx-16, and Game Gear**) have **capacitors that leak over time,** which can damage the motherboard.
- If your console **has no power or distorted audio,** it may need a **recap job.**

2 Yellowing Plastic? Try Retrobrighting

- Some older systems (like the **SNES and Apple computers**) **turn yellow over time** due to a chemical reaction in the plastic.
- Using a **hydrogen peroxide and UV light process** can **restore the original color.**

3 Controller Maintenance

- Buttons sticking? Open up the controller and **clean the contacts with alcohol.**
- Joysticks drifting? Many N64 controllers suffer from **wear and tear,** but **replacement joystick modules** can fix them.

Building Your Dream Retro Gaming Room

Once you've built a collection, it's time to **display and enjoy it.** A **dedicated retro gaming room** not only **keeps everything organized,** but also **creates an amazing gaming atmosphere**.

Essential Components of a Retro Gaming Room:

🎮 A Display That Works for Retro & Modern Games

- A **CRT TV** is perfect for that **authentic retro look,** but they're **getting harder to find.**
- A **high-quality gaming monitor with a RetroTINK** is a great modern alternative.

♦ Game Storage & Shelving

- Use **adjustable bookshelves** to display cartridges, cases, and manuals.
- Label your shelves by **console or generation** for easy access.

♟ A Multi-System Gaming Station

- If you have multiple consoles, a **high-quality AV switch** can make swapping between them seamless.
- Consider **FPGA-based systems like the Analogue Pocket or MiSTer** if you want multiple systems in one.

🎮 Comfortable Seating & Nostalgic Vibes

- A **comfy gaming chair or couch** makes long sessions better.
- Add **posters, neon lights, and memorabilia** to give your room that **classic arcade feel**.

Final Thoughts: Keeping Retro Games Alive

Collecting and restoring classic games isn't just about **owning old games**—it's about **preserving a piece of gaming history**. Whether you're a casual collector or someone hunting down the rarest finds, **there's nothing quite like holding a cartridge, booting up a classic console, and reliving those childhood memories.**

In the next chapter, we'll explore **how to introduce these classic games to your kids (or friends who missed out on them) and keep the retro gaming tradition alive for the next generation.**

Chapter 4: Bonding Over Video Games – Connecting with Your Kids Through Play

The First Time I Rented a PlayStation – A Trip to the Future

There was something special about renting video games in the '90s. It wasn't like today, where you just click a button and download a game instantly. Back then, video stores were sacred ground. Rows of VHS tapes lined the walls, and in the corner, behind a glass display case or a locked shelf, sat the video game section—our version of a treasure chest.

One Friday night, after begging my parents all week, we finally drove to the video store to rent something completely new: a PlayStation.

Yes, before most people owned one, you could rent an actual PlayStation console—a big, gray box that looked like a piece of alien technology compared to my old SNES and Genesis. It came in a hard plastic rental case, like something you'd expect to find in a military bunker, and inside, nestled in foam padding, was the controller.

That's when I saw them for the first time—the PlayStation's X, Square, Circle, and Triangle buttons.

Up until that point, every controller I had ever held had letters or numbers—A, B, C, L, R, Start, Select. But this? This was from another world. The symbols looked like something carved into an ancient ruin or a cryptic alien language meant for beings more advanced than us.

Even before I played a single game, I knew: this was the future.

And the first game I played? Tekken.

This wasn't some 2D fighter like *Street Fighter II*—this was fully 3D. Characters moved in depth, not just left and right. The fights felt more real, more fluid, more alive. I mashed buttons at first, but soon realized that memorizing the moves and combos was the real key to victory.

It was a mind-blowing experience, and one I still remember vividly. But looking back, the best part wasn't just discovering a new generation of gaming—it was playing it with friends and family, laughing, competing, and figuring it all out together.

Years later, gaming is still doing that—but now, it's my turn to pass the controller to the next generation.

Why Gaming Is a Great Way to Connect with Your Kids

We all know how quickly kids grow up—one day they're playing with action figures, the next they're glued to their phones. But gaming? Gaming is a bridge. It gives us a shared experience, a common language, something we can enjoy together no matter how old we get.

Why does gaming work so well for parent-child bonding?

1. It's Interactive (Unlike Watching TV or Movies)

- Watching a show together is great, but gaming isn't passive.
- You're solving problems, making choices, reacting together.
- Whether it's co-op teamwork or friendly competition, gaming creates shared moments in real time.

2. It Creates Natural Conversations

- Kids don't always open up when you ask them about their day. But while playing a game? The conversation flows.
- Whether you're working together in Minecraft or racing in Mario Kart, gaming creates opportunities to talk, joke, and connect without forcing it.

3. It Lets You Experience Their World

- If your kid is obsessed with Fortnite or Roblox, playing with them shows you what they love.
- Understanding their games helps build mutual respect—they get to teach you, and you get to share in their excitement.

4. It Helps Teach Important Life Skills

- Teamwork, patience, strategic thinking—gaming is more than just pressing buttons.
- Studies show that gaming can improve problem-solving, memory, and even social skills when played in a healthy way.

So, what are the best games to play with your kids?

The Best Modern Games for Co-op & Family Play

Gaming today is filled with amazing co-op experiences that let parents and kids team up, explore, and compete in ways that are fun for both generations.

Here are some of the best modern family-friendly games:

🎮 Mario Kart 8 Deluxe (Nintendo Switch)

- Fun for all ages, even beginners (thanks to auto-steering options).
- The ultimate family competition—fast, chaotic, and hilarious.
- Perfect for bonding through lighthearted rivalry.

🎮 Minecraft (All Platforms)

- Lets kids be creative, solve problems, and build their own worlds.
- Survival mode teaches teamwork and resource management.
- A great way to spend hours together without realizing it.

🎮 It Takes Two (PS4/PS5, Xbox, PC)

- One of the best co-op games ever made.
- Requires teamwork—every level is designed for two players to work together to solve puzzles and navigate challenges.
- A fantastic game for parents and kids to play side by side.

🎮 Overcooked! 2 (All Platforms)

- A chaotic but fun cooking game that requires cooperation and quick thinking.
- Perfect for families who like working together under pressure (or just enjoy yelling instructions at each other).

🎮 Super Smash Bros. Ultimate (Nintendo Switch)

- Simple enough for beginners to jump in, but deep enough to keep playing for years.
- A great mix of friendly competition and goofy fun.

These are just a few, but the key to picking a good family gaming experience is choosing something that lets you both have fun—without one player feeling left behind.

Introducing Your Kids to Retro Games (Without Them Rolling Their Eyes)

We all want our kids to appreciate the classics, but let's be real—when they're used to photo-realistic graphics and online multiplayer, convincing them to play an 8-bit game from the '80s isn't always easy.

How to Get Kids Interested in Retro Games:

1 Start with Games That Still Hold Up

- Some old games feel timeless, while others are just too frustrating for modern kids.
- Great starter retro games:
  - *Super Mario World (SNES)* – Still fun, still smooth, still iconic.
  - *Sonic the Hedgehog 2 (Genesis)* – Fast-paced enough to keep modern kids engaged.
  - *Tetris (Game Boy/NES)* – Easy to learn, still addictive today.

2 Use Modern Features Like Save States

- Classic games were brutally hard—giving kids a way to save progress makes them more approachable.
- Many modern retro collections (*Nintendo Switch Online, Sega Genesis Mini, etc.*) include save states and rewind features.

3 Make It a Fun Challenge

- Set up friendly competitions:
  - Who can beat the first level of *Super Mario Bros.* the fastest?
  - Who can get the highest score in Pac-Man?

4 Play Together & Share the Stories

- Kids love hearing why a game mattered to you—make it personal!
- Talk about what it was like playing these games when they were brand new.

Final Thoughts: Creating Gaming Memories That Last a Lifetime

In the end, it doesn't matter whether you're playing a modern co-op game or a classic from your childhood—what matters is the time spent together.

Someday, our kids might be the ones introducing their own children to the games they grew up with. And if we do it right, they'll remember these moments not just as "gaming time," but as some of the best memories with their parents.

So grab a controller, pick a game, and get ready to make gaming history together.

Chapter 5: Managing Screen Time Without Ruining the Fun

Gaming is one of the greatest joys of modern entertainment, but like anything, too much of a good thing can become a problem. As parents, we want our kids to enjoy video games, but we also don't want them to get lost in them at the expense of school, friendships, and real-world experiences.

I know this struggle first hand—because I once fell deep into the gaming rabbit hole myself.

When *Grand Theft Auto* Almost Flunked Me Out of College

I'll never forget the day *Grand Theft Auto III* dropped for PlayStation 2. Up until that point, open-world games were limited, structured, and predictable—but this? This was a living, breathing city, a world where you could do whatever you wanted.

At first, I thought I'd just play for an hour or two between classes. But soon, the game took over my life.

- I skipped studying because I was running missions instead.
- I told myself, *"Just one more hour"*—but then I'd look at the clock, and it was 4 AM.
- I even dreamed in GTA, plotting heists in my sleep.

By the time midterms rolled around, I was dangerously close to failing. I hadn't studied, hadn't turned in assignments, and I was running on zero sleep. It hit me like a ton of bricks—I was obsessed.

That was the moment I realized gaming needed balance. I didn't need to give up video games, but I had to control them before they controlled me.

Now, as a parent, I want to make sure my kids never fall into that same trap. And the good news? There's a way to strike that balance without making gaming feel like the enemy.

Striking the Balance Between Gaming and Real Life

Video games are a huge part of our kids' world—and instead of fighting against them, the goal is to integrate gaming into a well-balanced life.

1. The "Gaming as Dessert" Mindset

- Think of gaming like dessert—something to enjoy, but not the main course.
- School, homework, outdoor play, and family time are the "meal", and gaming is the treat that comes after.
- This simple analogy helps kids see gaming as part of a bigger routine, rather than an all-consuming activity.

2. Gaming Shouldn't Replace Other Activities

- It's fine for kids to have favorite hobbies, but gaming shouldn't be their only hobby.
- Encourage them to balance gaming with sports, reading, creative projects, and real-world adventures.
- A good rule of thumb: Make sure for every hour of gaming, they're engaging in at least one other non-screen activity.

3. Teach Self-Management Instead of Just Enforcing Rules

- Instead of saying "You're only allowed 1 hour", involve kids in managing their own screen time.
- Ask questions like:
    - "How do you think gaming fits into your day?"
    - "What's a good way to make sure you're still getting your schoolwork done?"
- Kids are more likely to follow rules they helped create.

Setting Gaming Rules That Actually Work

One of the hardest parts of managing screen time is setting boundaries without making gaming feel like a punishment. The goal is to establish rules that are fair, enforceable, and flexible enough to fit real life.

1. Set Clear Limits (And Stick to Them)

- Consistent rules make gaming expectations clear.
- Examples of screen time limits that work:
  - Weekdays: Homework first, then up to 1 hour of gaming.
  - Weekends: Free play time but still balanced with other activities.
  - No screens during meals or before bedtime (this helps with sleep and focus).

2. Use Timers & Natural Break Points

- Many games don't have clear stopping points, so set limits based on in-game milestones:
  - "You can play until you finish this mission."
  - "You can play until the end of this round/match."
- Using timers (like a kitchen timer or in-game reminders) helps kids pace themselves.

3. Encourage Social Gaming Over Solo Play

- Playing with friends or family is a healthier way to enjoy gaming than playing alone for hours.
- Co-op games, party games, and online multiplayer with real-life friends make gaming more interactive and less isolating.

4. Have "Tech-Free Zones"

- Set specific no-screen areas in the house (like bedrooms or the dinner table).
- This ensures kids get a break from screens without making gaming feel "banned."

How to Encourage Creativity and Learning Through Gaming

Not all screen time is equal—some games encourage creativity, problem-solving, and even real-world skills. The trick is helping kids engage with gaming in ways that benefit them beyond just entertainment.

1. Choose Games That Foster Creativity

- Some games spark imagination and teach valuable skills:
  - *Minecraft* – Creativity, building, teamwork.
  - *Super Mario Maker* – Game design and critical thinking.
  - *Kerbal Space Program* – Physics and problem-solving.
- Encourage kids to create, not just consume.
  - Let them design their own levels in Mario Maker or build their dream world in Minecraft.

2. Use Gaming to Encourage Problem-Solving

- Puzzle-based games like *Portal 2*, *Zelda*, or *The Witness* teach logical thinking and patience.
- Strategy games like *Civilization* or *Stardew Valley* develop planning and resource management skills.

3. Explore the Educational Side of Gaming

- Many games combine learning with fun:
  - *Oregon Trail* – History.
  - *Typing of the Dead* – Typing skills.
  - *Assassin's Creed Discovery Mode* – Historical exploration.
- Even games that aren't explicitly educational can teach valuable lessons:
  - *Role-playing games (RPGs) encourage reading and decision-making.*
  - *Multiplayer games teach teamwork and communication.*

4. Get Kids Interested in Game Development

- If your child loves gaming, introduce them to how games are made.
- Tools like Scratch, Roblox Studio, and Unity let kids experiment with game design.
- Coding and digital creativity can turn a gaming passion into a future career.

Final Thoughts: Gaming Should Be a Fun, Healthy Part of Life

Looking back at my *Grand Theft Auto III* college obsession, I realize gaming wasn't the problem—the lack of balance was.

I could have set time limits, I could have taken breaks, and I definitely could have studied more. But instead, I got completely sucked into the game world, ignoring everything else.

Now, as a parent, I want my kids to love video games just as much as I do—but in a way that's healthy, balanced, and enriching.

Gaming isn't the enemy. Too much of it, at the expense of real life, is.

If we approach it the right way, video games can be an amazing tool for learning, bonding, and creativity—without ever becoming a problem.

And that's the ultimate goal: enjoying gaming as part of a well-rounded life—one where we play, learn, and grow together.

Chapter 6: Keeping Up with Modern Games (Without Getting Lost)

Gaming has evolved a lot since the days of blowing into cartridges and memorizing cheat codes from magazines. Modern games are bigger, more complex, and often designed around online multiplayer—which can feel overwhelming for those of us who grew up with simpler, more straightforward gaming experiences.

For many Gen X gamers, keeping up with the latest trends isn't just about staying informed—it's about finding games that are actually fun without requiring a second job's worth of practice. As much as we might love the idea of jumping into the newest first-person shooter (FPS) or battle royale, the reality is that our reflexes aren't quite what they used to be, and let's be honest—we don't have time to grind for hours just to be competitive.

I learned this the hard way.

The Moment I Realized I Wasn't as Fast as I Used to Be

There was a time when I could hold my own in multiplayer FPS games. Back in the days of *Quake*, *Unreal Tournament*, and even early *Call of Duty*, I had the skills to go toe-to-toe with just about anyone. My reaction time was sharp, my aim was steady, and I could predict my opponents' moves like I was reading their minds.

Fast forward to today.

I tried jumping into *Call of Duty: Warzone* and *Apex Legends*, and... let's just say it didn't go well.

- I'd drop into the match, scramble for a weapon, and get eliminated in seconds before I even knew what hit me.
- The players I was up against were faster, more precise, and seemingly had ESP, knowing exactly where I was before I even saw them.
- The learning curve? Brutal. The time investment required to get good? More than I had to spare.

I quickly realized something: I don't have the patience—or the reflexes—to keep up with 15-year-olds who spend 8 hours a day perfecting their aim.

So instead of banging my head against the wall trying to reclaim my FPS glory days, I turned to Steam to see what other options were out there. That's when I discovered games like *The Forest* and *7 Days to Die*—games that offered immersive, strategic gameplay without demanding instant reaction times and constant practice.

And you know what? I had just as much fun, if not more.

Understanding Modern Gaming Trends Without Getting Overwhelmed

Modern gaming can feel intimidating, especially with all the new genres, business models, and online components. Here's a quick breakdown of the biggest trends and what they mean for Gen X gamers:

1. Battle Royales – The Survival of the Quickest

- Games like *Fortnite*, *Warzone*, and *Apex Legends* throw dozens of players into a massive arena where only one team or player survives.
- Matches are fast, unpredictable, and highly competitive.
- They require constant practice—which can be frustrating if you don't have time to keep up.
- Best for: Gamers who love fast-paced action and online competition.
- Avoid if: You don't have time to keep up with constantly changing weapons, mechanics, and maps.

2. Open-World RPGs – The Ultimate "Play at Your Own Pace" Experience

- These games let you explore massive worlds at your own speed.
- Examples: *The Witcher 3*, *Elden Ring*, *Horizon: Zero Dawn*.
- They reward patience, exploration, and immersion rather than lightning-fast reflexes.
- Best for: Gamers who love deep stories, character progression, and adventure.
- Avoid if: You prefer short, fast-paced sessions over long, drawn-out gameplay.

3. Survival Games – The Thinking Gamer's FPS Alternative

- These games mix crafting, exploration, and strategy with some action.
- Examples: *The Forest*, *7 Days to Die*, *Green Hell*, *Valheim*.
- They don't require super-fast reaction times—instead, they reward patience, planning, and teamwork.
- Best for: Gamers who want immersive experiences without needing to "git gud" at aiming.
- Avoid if: You prefer instant action over slow-building tension.

4. Co-op & Social Games – Playing Together Without the Toxicity

- Games built around cooperation rather than competition.
- Examples: *Sea of Thieves*, *Phasmophobia*, *Deep Rock Galactic*.

- They're fun with friends, but casual enough that you don't need hours of practice.
- Best for: Gamers who enjoy laughing and strategizing with friends instead of competing.
- Avoid if: You prefer solo experiences over teamwork.

The Best Modern Games That Still Feel Old-School

If you grew up on classic games, you'll be happy to know that some modern titles capture that old-school magic while still embracing today's technology.

🎮 Doom Eternal – *Fast, single-player FPS action like the old days, but with modern polish.*
🎮 Hollow Knight – *A beautiful, modern take on classic Metroidvania-style exploration.*
🎮 Streets of Rage 4 – *Old-school beat-em-up gameplay, modern visuals.*
🎮 Shovel Knight – *8-bit aesthetics, but deep and rewarding gameplay.*
🎮 Diablo IV – *Classic dungeon-crawling, loot-grinding goodness.*

These games bring the fun of classic gaming into the modern age—without forcing you to learn an entirely new way to play.

How to Find Games That Fit Into a Busy Life

Let's face it—as we get older, our free time shrinks. Between work, family, and responsibilities, it's tough to find time for huge, time-sucking games.

Here's how to find games that fit your lifestyle without demanding your soul:

1. Look for Games with Quick Play Sessions

- Great choices: *Hades, Dead Cells, Rocket League.*
- These games let you jump in, have fun, and log off without a huge commitment.

2. Focus on Games with Pause & Save Anytime Options

- Nothing is worse than getting interrupted and losing progress.
- Great choices: *Slay the Spire, Stardew Valley, Into the Breach.*

3. Find Co-op Games That Don't Require Constant Practice

- Some multiplayer games are fun even if you only play occasionally.
- Great choices: *Deep Rock Galactic*, *Sea of Thieves*, *Left 4 Dead 2*.

4. Explore Turn-Based Games That Let You Play at Your Own Speed

- Great choices: *Civilization VI*, *XCOM 2*, *Final Fantasy Tactics*.
- No need to rush—take your time, think, and play on your own schedule.

Final Thoughts: Gaming Can Still Be Amazing Without the Grind

Getting older doesn't mean we have to stop gaming—it just means we have to find games that match where we are in life.

For me, stepping away from hyper-competitive FPS games and into more strategic, immersive games like *The Forest* and *7 Days to Die* was a game-changer. I can still experience the thrill, the challenge, and the adventure—just on my own terms.

And that's the best part of gaming today: No matter your age, skill level, or time constraints, there's always a game out there that fits your life perfectly. You just have to find it.

Chapter 7: Online Gaming Without the Toxicity

Online gaming has come a long way from the early days of dial-up connections, LAN parties, and Medal of Honor: Allied Assault deathmatches. The ability to jump into a game at any time, team up with friends across the world, and experience multiplayer battles at an unprecedented scale is one of the greatest things about modern gaming.

But let's be honest—it's also one of the worst.

For many Gen X gamers, online gaming today feels more exhausting than enjoyable. Between rage-fueled players, immature trash talk, and communities that seem designed to make newcomers feel unwelcome, it's easy to wonder if we've outgrown online gaming—or if online gaming has outgrown us.

The good news? There are ways to enjoy online games without dealing with toxic players. It's just about knowing where to look, how to avoid the worst parts of online culture, and which games actually encourage positive interactions.

When Nate and I Were the Toxic Ones – The Brutal Days of *Medal of Honor* Online

I have to admit, there was a time when I was part of the problem.

Back in the early 2000s, my buddy Nate and I spent countless nights dominating in *Medal of Honor: Allied Assault* online. This was before modern matchmaking, before voice moderation, before "report" buttons. It was pure, unfiltered, no-holds-barred multiplayer warfare.

And we took full advantage of it.

- We weren't just winning matches—we were destroying entire teams, making it our personal mission to wipe the floor with them.
- Our trash talk? Relentless. We said things in chat that, looking back, were definitely not politically correct—things we wouldn't say today.
- We thrived on making opponents rage-quit—if we weren't getting hate messages in chat, we weren't playing hard enough.

At the time, it was just part of the culture. Online gaming was like the Wild West—no rules, no consequences, just chaos. And honestly? It was fun.

But as the years went on, something changed.

We got older. We had jobs, responsibilities, families. Suddenly, talking trash to a bunch of teenagers online wasn't entertaining anymore—it was exhausting.

And when we started playing online games again, we realized something:

- We didn't want to destroy people anymore—we just wanted to have fun.
- We didn't want to deal with toxic players—we wanted to play with people who actually enjoyed the game.
- We weren't trying to prove ourselves anymore—we just wanted to relax.

So, we made a choice: Find online games that let us play how we wanted—without all the drama.

The Best Online Games for Casual Players

Not every online game is about competitive rankings and ego-driven trash talk. If you're looking for games that let you enjoy multiplayer without requiring constant practice or dealing with toxic communities, here are some of the best options:

🎮 Co-op & Team-Based Games (Where Players Actually Work Together)

▪ Deep Rock Galactic (*PC, Xbox*)

- A co-op game where you and your team play as space dwarves, mining alien caves and fighting off creatures.
- No PvP, no competition—just teamwork and fun.
- Community is notoriously friendly and helpful.

▪ Sea of Thieves (*PC, Xbox*)

- Open-world pirate game where you sail, find treasure, and battle sea monsters.
- While PvP exists, most of the community just enjoys sailing together.
- Perfect for laughing, adventuring, and playing at your own pace.

▪ Monster Hunter: World / Rise (*PC, PlayStation, Switch*)

- A team-based game where you hunt giant monsters together.
- No trash talk, no stress—just teamwork and strategy.
- Feels more rewarding than competitive shooters since it's all about skillful combat and cooperation.

🎮 Casual Multiplayer Games (For When You Just Want to Have Fun)

▪ Rocket League (*PC, PlayStation, Xbox, Switch*)

- Car soccer that is easy to learn but hard to master.
- Five-minute matches make it great for short play sessions.
- While ranked mode has competitive players, casual play is low-stress and fun.

▪ Fall Guys (*PC, PlayStation, Xbox, Switch*)

- A wacky, obstacle-course battle royale where you just try to survive hilarious challenges.
- No toxic players, no intense competition—just goofy fun.

▪ Golf With Your Friends (*PC, Console*)

- Mini-golf that's hilarious and unpredictable.
- No stress, no ranking system—just relaxing multiplayer chaos.

Avoiding the Worst of Online Gaming Culture

Even in great games, toxic players exist. Here's how to enjoy online gaming without letting negativity ruin the experience.

1. Turn Off Public Voice Chat (Or Use Party Chat Only)

- The fastest way to avoid trash talk and toxicity is to mute the public chat completely.
- Use party chat with friends only for a much better experience.

2. Play With Friends Whenever Possible

- Online gaming is always better with friends—even just one other person makes a huge difference.
- Toxic players are easier to ignore when you have a group of teammates you trust.

3. Avoid Ultra-Competitive Modes (Unless You're Ready for the Stress)

- Ranked/competitive playlists tend to bring out the worst in players.
- Stick to casual or unranked modes if you just want to have fun.

4. Report and Block Toxic Players

- Every modern game has a report and mute function—use it.
- Blocking players prevents them from messaging or joining your matches.

Finding Gaming Communities That Actually Feel Welcoming

The best way to enjoy online gaming is to find a good group of players who share your mindset.

Where to Find Positive Gaming Communities:

● Reddit & Discord – Many games have subreddits and Discord servers filled with casual, friendly players looking for teammates.
● Facebook Groups – Believe it or not, Facebook has solid gaming groups for parents and casual gamers.
● In-Game Guilds & Clans – Many games (especially MMOs) have casual, social guilds that don't take things too seriously.

Signs of a Good Gaming Community:

■ Encourages new players instead of mocking them.
■ Focuses on fun, not just "winning."
■ Has clear rules against harassment & toxicity.
■ Supports casual gamers, not just hardcore veterans.

Final Thoughts: Making Online Gaming Fun Again

Back in the *Medal of Honor* days, Nate and I played online games to win at all costs. But now? We play to enjoy the experience.

We don't need to crush other players to have fun. We don't need to deal with toxic communities just to play a game.

Instead, we've found that gaming is at its best when you surround yourself with good people, play games that match your style, and focus on fun instead of frustration.

If you love online gaming but hate the toxicity that comes with it, remember:

● Avoid the bad communities.
■ Find the good ones.
● Play the games that let you have fun on your own terms.

Because at the end of the day, gaming should be an escape—not a headache.

Chapter 8: Next-Level Gaming – VR, Streaming, and What's Coming Next

Gaming has never stood still. From arcades and home consoles to online multiplayer and esports, each generation has seen a leap forward. But right now? We're on the edge of another major transformation—one that includes virtual reality, cloud gaming, and content creation becoming as mainstream as gaming itself.

For many Gen X gamers, these changes can feel exciting but overwhelming. We grew up with controllers in our hands and cartridges in our consoles—so concepts like wearing a headset to step inside a game or playing a game that isn't even installed on our device might feel a little like science fiction.

But the truth is, gaming's future is more accessible than it seems. Whether you're interested in exploring VR, subscribing to a massive library of games, or even trying out streaming for fun, there's a way to embrace modern gaming without losing what we love about the classics.

Is VR Worth It for Gen X Gamers?

The First Time I Tried VR – A Vacation in Wisconsin Dells

For years, I was curious about virtual reality, but I never made the leap to buy a headset. It seemed expensive, and I wasn't convinced it would be more than just a fun gimmick. But one summer, while visiting Wisconsin Dells, I finally gave it a shot.

We found this VR arcade in one of the touristy parts of town. The walls were covered with images of futuristic headsets, sci-fi worlds, and intense-looking action games. I figured, *why not?* It was the perfect chance to see what all the fuss was about.

The employee strapped a VR headset on me, handed me controllers, and loaded up a game like *Superhot VR*.

The moment the game started, I was completely blown away.

- Instead of just watching a game on a screen, I was inside it—dodging bullets, grabbing objects in mid-air, and moving my whole body to interact with the world.
- It wasn't just about quick reflexes—it was about strategy, timing, and full immersion.
- I found myself ducking, leaning, and physically reacting to everything happening around me.

By the time I took off the headset, I knew: VR was the real deal.

But is it worth buying a headset for home use?

The Pros & Cons of VR Gaming

■ Unmatched Immersion – VR truly transports you into the game in a way nothing else can.

■ Physical & Active Gaming – It's one of the few gaming platforms where you move your whole body.

■ Unique Gaming Experiences – From horror games where you feel trapped inside the action to meditative games that make you feel like you're floating in space.

✕ Expensive Entry Cost – A solid VR setup (like Meta Quest 3 or PlayStation VR2) isn't cheap.

✕ Motion Sickness Can Be an Issue – Some players struggle with nausea, especially in fast-moving games.

✕ Space Requirements – You need room to move around, which can be tricky in small spaces.

Is VR Worth It?

If you're the kind of gamer who loves trying new technology, exploring immersive experiences, or enjoys more active gaming, then VR is absolutely worth checking out. However, if you prefer relaxed gaming, long RPGs, or short gaming sessions, you might not get as much out of it.

Cloud Gaming, Game Subscriptions, and How the Industry is Changing

The way we buy and play games is shifting fast. Instead of buying individual games, more players are turning to gaming subscriptions and cloud services—where you can play a massive library of titles without needing to own a powerful console.

The Big Players in Cloud Gaming & Subscription Services

♣ Xbox Game Pass Ultimate – Gives you access to hundreds of games for a monthly fee, including brand-new releases on day one.

♣ PlayStation Plus Premium – Offers classic PlayStation games, cloud streaming, and exclusive discounts.

♣ GeForce Now – Streams PC games at high settings, even on weaker hardware.

♣ Amazon Luna – A newer streaming platform that lets you play on any device without downloading.

The Pros & Cons of Cloud Gaming & Subscriptions

■ Instant Access to Games – No more waiting for downloads—jump in and play immediately.
■ More Affordable Than Buying Individual Games – A single subscription can give you hundreds of games.
■ No Need for Expensive Hardware – Cloud gaming lets you play high-end games on budget laptops or even smartphones.

✗ You Don't Own the Games – If a game leaves the service, you lose access to it.
✗ Requires Fast Internet – If your connection isn't great, cloud gaming won't work well.
✗ Cloud Gaming Still Has Lag – Even with improvements, streamed games still feel slightly less responsive than playing locally.

Is It Worth It?

If you play a lot of games and like the idea of always having something new to try, a subscription like Game Pass is a fantastic deal. If you prefer to own your games or don't have reliable internet, cloud gaming might not be a great fit yet.

How to Get Into Streaming or Content Creation as a Midlife Gamer

Many Gen X gamers assume that game streaming and content creation is a young person's game—but that couldn't be further from the truth. More and more midlife gamers are finding an audience online, whether through Twitch streaming, YouTube videos, or gaming podcasts.

Why Older Gamers Are Entering Content Creation

- Authenticity is in demand – Viewers are tired of over-the-top, fake personalities and are looking for real, relatable people.
- Older gamers have experience & perspective – We grew up with gaming and have a lot of stories to share.
- Casual & relaxed content is popular – Not everyone wants high-energy esports content—many just want chill, enjoyable gameplay.

How to Start Streaming or Making Videos

Pick a Platform

- Twitch – Best for live streaming & audience interaction.
- YouTube – Great for game reviews, playthroughs, or discussion videos.
- TikTok / Instagram Reels – Short clips work great for casual gaming content.

Choose a Content Style

- Let's Plays – Play through games and talk about your experiences.
- Gaming Discussions – Share your thoughts on gaming trends, nostalgia, and industry news.
- Retro Gaming Content – There's a huge audience for players who love classic games.

Keep It Simple

- You don't need fancy equipment—a basic webcam and mic are enough to start.
- Use OBS Studio (free software) to capture and stream gameplay.
- Play what you love, and your passion will shine through.

What's Coming Next in Gaming?

● AI-Generated Games – AI will create dynamic, ever-changing game worlds.

● More Cross-Platform Play – Future games will let you play with friends on any device.

● VR & AR Becoming Mainstream – Virtual reality will blend with real-world augmented reality experiences.

● Gaming Without Consoles – Cloud gaming may eventually replace physical gaming hardware.

Final Thoughts: Embracing the Future of Gaming

Just because gaming is changing fast doesn't mean we have to be left behind. Whether it's trying VR, subscribing to a massive game library, or even experimenting with streaming, there's something new and exciting for every kind of gamer.

The key is to keep gaming on your own terms—embracing new experiences without losing sight of what made us fall in love with games in the first place.

Conclusion: Gaming is a Lifelong Hobby

For many of us in Generation X, gaming has been a part of our lives for as long as we can remember. From arcades and 8-bit consoles to online multiplayer and VR, we've grown up alongside gaming's evolution. But as we get older, it's easy to wonder: *Is gaming still for us?*

The truth is, gaming doesn't have an age limit. Whether you're playing casually, diving into deep single-player stories, or just using games as a way to unwind, there's no "right" way to be a gamer.

Sure, we might not have as much free time as we did in our teenage years, and our reflexes might not be as sharp as they were back in the Medal of Honor days, but gaming is still just as enjoyable—if not more—because we now appreciate it differently.

Why You're Never "Too Old" for Gaming

One of the biggest myths about gaming is that it's just for kids. But if you look at the numbers, that couldn't be further from the truth.

- The average gamer is around 35 years old, according to industry studies.
- Millions of Gen X and older millennials still play regularly, whether it's solo RPGs, casual mobile games, or online multiplayer.
- Gaming isn't just about fast reflexes—it's about strategy, problem-solving, creativity, and relaxation.

Think about it: Do people "outgrow" watching movies or reading books? Of course not! Gaming is just another form of entertainment—one that happens to be interactive.

How to Balance Gaming with Everything Else in Life

As much as we love gaming, it's easy to lose track of time—especially with today's open-world games, online experiences, and endless side quests.

How I Learned to Set Timers in *Farm Simulator*

One night, I sat down to play just a little bit of *Farm Simulator*. I told myself, *I'll harvest a few fields, check on my animals, and call it a night.*

But you know how it goes.

- One task turned into another.
- I started optimizing my crop rotation.
- Then I realized I needed to buy a new harvester.
- Then I got into customizing my farm layout.

By the time I looked at the clock, three hours had passed, and I had completely lost track of time.

After that, I decided: No more accidental all-night gaming sessions.

Now, when I play games like *Farm Simulator*—or any game that tends to pull me in for "just one more thing"—I set timers.

- A one-hour timer reminds me to pause and check if I should keep playing.
- A "hard stop" alarm ensures I don't go overboard on nights when I have things to do the next morning.

It's a small change, but it's helped me enjoy gaming without letting it interfere with the rest of my life.

Other Tips for Balancing Gaming & Real Life

■ Make Gaming a Reward – Finish your to-do list, then relax with a game guilt-free.
■ Schedule Gaming Time – Treat it like a hobby, not a time-filler.
■ Play Games That Fit Your Life – Pick games that match your available time and energy level.
■ Use Break Reminders – If you're gaming for long sessions, take breaks to stretch and reset.

The Best Ways to Keep the Gaming Spirit Alive

As we get older, gaming might not be the center of our lives like it was when we were younger, but that doesn't mean we have to give it up. Instead, we can find new ways to enjoy it while fitting it into our current lifestyle.

1. Play Games That Fit Your Interests Now

Your gaming tastes might have evolved over the years, and that's okay!

- Maybe you used to love intense FPS games, but now you prefer immersive survival sims (*The Forest*, *7 Days to Die*).
- Maybe you were a huge fan of fast-paced action, but now you enjoy story-driven RPGs (*The Witcher 3*, *Red Dead Redemption 2*).
- Maybe you used to compete online, but now you prefer co-op games where you can work together with friends instead of fighting against them.

2. Share Gaming with Family & Friends

One of the best ways to keep gaming enjoyable is to share it with others.

■ Play with your kids – Show them the games you loved growing up, or join them in their favorite modern games.

🎮 Reconnect with old gaming buddies – A quick co-op game can be a great way to stay in touch with friends.

♟ Introduce gaming to non-gamer friends or partners – Casual games like *Mario Kart*, *Jackbox Party Packs*, or *Minecraft* make it easy for anyone to join in.

3. Explore New Gaming Tech Without Feeling Pressured

Gaming is changing fast, but you don't have to keep up with everything.

- If VR sounds fun, try it out—but don't feel like you *need* to buy a headset.
- If cloud gaming sounds convenient, test a free trial before diving in.
- If streaming or making content sounds interesting, experiment without worrying about being an expert.

Gaming is not about trends—it's about what brings you joy.

Final Thoughts: Gaming Will Always Be There

No matter how life changes, gaming is one of those rare hobbies that stays with you. It's something you can come back to whenever you need an escape, a challenge, or just a little fun.

Some of us may game less than we used to, but that's okay. The important thing is that when we do pick up the controller, we enjoy every minute of it.

So whether you're playing for five minutes or five hours, just remember:

- ♣ Gaming is never a waste of time when it makes you happy.
- 🎮 There's no such thing as "too old" for gaming.
- ⧗ Find a balance that works for you, and keep gaming on your own terms.

Because at the end of the day, once a gamer, always a gamer.

Bonus Content: Essential Resources for Gen X Gamers

Whether you're rediscovering your favorite classics, looking for modern games that still capture that old-school magic, or diving deeper into the gaming world, this bonus section is here to help.

Inside, you'll find:
- ✔ A checklist of must-play retro and modern games
- ✔ A guide to buying affordable retro gaming gear
- ✔ A list of the best YouTube channels and podcasts for Gen X gamers—including my personal favorite at the moment, Farmer Cop for *Farm Simulator 25* tips and strategies.

Must-Play Retro and Modern Games

Some games are timeless, while others push the boundaries of modern gaming. If you're looking to revisit old favorites or try something new, this list covers the best of both worlds.

🎮 Essential Retro Games Every Gen X Gamer Should Play (or Replay)

If you grew up in the '80s and '90s, these classics probably played a huge role in your gaming life. Whether you're reliving the nostalgia or discovering what you missed, these games still hold up today.

🎮 NES & SNES Era
■ *Super Mario Bros. 3* (NES) – One of the greatest platformers ever made.
■ *The Legend of Zelda: A Link to the Past* (SNES) – Still one of the best action RPGs of all time.
■ *Mega Man 2* (NES) – A perfect balance of challenge and fun.
■ *Final Fantasy VI* (SNES) – Classic storytelling and unforgettable characters.
■ *Super Metroid* (SNES) – The game that defined exploration-based platformers.

🎮 Sega Genesis & PlayStation 1/2 Era
■ *Sonic the Hedgehog 2* (Genesis) – Fast-paced, high-energy platforming at its best.
■ *Street Fighter II* (Arcade/SNES/Genesis) – The king of fighting games.
■ *Castlevania: Symphony of the Night* (PS1) – The reason we call the genre "Metroidvania."
■ *Tony Hawk's Pro Skater 2* (PS1) – Nothing beats pulling off a perfect combo.
■ *Grand Theft Auto: San Andreas* (PS2) – A groundbreaking open-world experience.

🎮 Must-Play Modern Games for Gen X Gamers

If you love classic gaming but want something with modern polish, these games capture the spirit of old-school gaming with updated mechanics and visuals.

🎮 Modern Games with Old-School Vibes
■ *Hollow Knight* – A masterpiece for Metroidvania fans.
■ *Doom Eternal* – The perfect mix of classic fast-paced FPS gameplay and modern graphics.
■ *Shovel Knight* – A love letter to NES-era platformers.
■ *Streets of Rage 4* – A fantastic modern beat-em-up.
■ *Resident Evil 2 Remake* – Classic survival horror reborn with stunning visuals.

🎮 Great Games for Casual & Busy Gamers
■ *Farm Simulator 25* – The perfect laid-back game, with deep mechanics for those who love strategy.
■ *The Witcher 3* – A sprawling open-world RPG you can play at your own pace.

■ *7 Days to Die* – A survival horror sandbox that doesn't demand fast reflexes but rewards creativity.
■ *No Man's Sky* – A game built for exploration without stress.
■ *Deep Rock Galactic* – Co-op fun without toxic competition.

A Guide to Buying Affordable Retro Gaming Gear

Retro gaming doesn't have to break the bank—if you know where to look. Whether you want to collect physical cartridges or play classics on modern hardware, here are some tips for getting the best deals.

Where to Buy Retro Games Without Overpaying

■ Local Game Stores – Some independent game shops still sell used retro games at fair prices.
■ Flea Markets & Thrift Stores – Occasionally, you can find hidden gems that people don't realize are valuable.
■ Garage Sales & Estate Sales – Some people sell off old gaming collections without knowing their worth.
■ Facebook Marketplace / Craigslist / OfferUp – Great for finding local deals and avoiding shipping costs.
■ eBay – You'll find almost any retro game here, but beware of overpriced listings.

Modern Alternatives for Playing Retro Games

If you don't want to hunt down original consoles, here are some great ways to play classic games affordably:

🪝 Mini Consoles – Systems like the SNES Classic, Sega Genesis Mini, and PlayStation Classic offer plug-and-play retro experiences with built-in games.
🪝 FPGA Consoles (Analogue Pocket, MiSTer) – These systems replicate classic hardware perfectly, making them ideal for purists.
🪝 Retro Game Handhelds (Anbernic, Retroid Pocket) – Portable all-in-one devices that let you play multiple classic systems on the go.
🪝 Emulation on PC & Steam Deck – If you don't mind digital copies, emulation is the most affordable way to play classics.

The Best Gaming YouTube Channels and Podcasts for Gen X Gamers

With so much gaming content online, it can be hard to find channels and podcasts that actually cater to Gen X gamers. Here's a list of some of the best resources for gaming news, nostalgia, and deep dives into strategy.

🎥 YouTube Channels Worth Following

◼ **Farmer Cop** – My personal favorite at the moment—his Farm Simulator 25 tutorials and strategies are incredibly useful. If you want to maximize your farm's efficiency without wasting time, this is the channel to watch.

◼ **MetalJesusRocks** – Perfect for retro gaming collectors and hidden gem recommendations.
◼ **Spawn Wave** – Great for gaming news, reviews, and hardware breakdowns.
◼ **John Hancock** – Covers classic gaming and rare retro finds.
◼ **My Life in Gaming** – Deep dives into retro game hardware and display options.

🎙 Podcasts for Gen X Gamers

🎧 **Retronauts** – One of the best deep-dive retro gaming podcasts.
🎧 **The SpawnCast** – Weekly gaming news and discussion.
🎧 **Triple Click** – Great discussions on gaming culture and industry trends.
🎧 **The Retro Hour** – Features interviews with gaming legends and discussions on classic games.
🎧 **Gamers With Jobs** – Perfect for busy adults who still love gaming.

Final Thoughts: Keeping Gaming Fun & Affordable

No matter how much gaming evolves, the love for great games stays the same. Whether you're revisiting childhood classics, exploring modern experiences that feel old-school, or diving into content that helps you play smarter, there are endless ways to stay engaged without feeling overwhelmed.

The key is to find what works for you.

- Want to play retro games on modern devices? There's an option for that.
- Want to discover new games that fit a busy lifestyle? They exist.
- Want to watch or listen to gaming content that actually speaks to our generation? Plenty of choices.

At the end of the day, gaming is about enjoyment—whether it's casual, nostalgic, or a brand-new experience.

So grab a controller, pick a game, and keep playing on your own terms.

Bonus Chapter: Mortal Kombat II – The Ultimate '90s Arcade Battleground

I finished writing this book, closed my laptop, and leaned back in my chair, feeling pretty good about covering all the major games that shaped my love for gaming.

And then it hit me.

Like a bolt of lightning straight from Raiden himself, I realized I forgot to mention the one game that probably stole more of my quarters than any other. The game that had me hunched over arcade cabinets in bowling alleys, scanning gaming magazines for secret move lists, and memorizing absurdly long button combinations to pull off insane transformations and brutal finishers.

A game where I could turn my opponent into a baby, give them a birthday cake, or—more importantly—rip them apart in a spectacularly gruesome Fatality that made the entire arcade cheer.

The mid-'90s were a barbaric time, and I wouldn't have had it any other way.

Of course, I'm talking about Mortal Kombat II—in my opinion, the greatest multiplayer fighting game of its era.

Mortal Kombat II – The Wildest Arcade Experience of the '90s

Back in the early '90s, fighting games were already becoming a phenomenon, thanks to *Street Fighter II*. But *Mortal Kombat*? That was a different beast entirely. It wasn't about finesse and competitive balance—it was about pure spectacle, shock value, and absolutely crushing your opponent in the most dramatic way possible.

By the time Mortal Kombat II hit the arcades in the early 90's, the series had already built a reputation for its insane violence, over-the-top characters, and that unforgettable "Finish Him!" moment. But *Mortal Kombat II* took everything the first game did and made it better.

- Faster, smoother gameplay
- More characters with deeper movesets

- Hidden secrets, ridiculous Easter eggs, and multiple types of finishers
- Graphics that felt light-years ahead of other fighting games at the time

And, of course, the Fatalities.

The Art of Memorizing Fatalities (And Failing Spectacularly in Public)

Pulling off a Fatality in *Mortal Kombat II* wasn't just a cool finishing move—it was a status symbol.

If you knew how to execute a Fatality on command, you weren't just some random kid in the arcade—you were a legend. People gathered around to watch, and if you nailed it, you might get actual applause from strangers.

But if you messed up?

- You'd be standing there, frantically inputting a complex string of commands, only to accidentally throw a weak punch as your opponent keeled over.
- The arcade crowd would groan in disappointment.
- Your opponent, still stunned from losing, would laugh at your failure.

And you'd have to live with the shame of knowing you could've ripped their head off in front of everyone, but instead, you just gave them a light tap to the chest.

This was arcade pressure at its peak.

The Ultimate Multiplayer Experience – The Rivalries and the Glory

Arcade gaming in the '90s was a different world. There was no online matchmaking, no skill-based ranking system, no trash-talking over headsets. If you wanted to prove yourself, you had to step up to the machine, put in your quarter, and face someone in real life.

And *Mortal Kombat II* brought out the best—and worst—in everyone.

- If you won, you stayed at the machine, stacking quarters on the edge to mark your dominance.

- If you lost, you had to walk away and wait for another shot—sometimes watching your rival destroy opponent after opponent, knowing you were next in line.
- There were unwritten arcade rules, like no spamming moves too much (or you'd get dirty looks), but also no mercy when it came to finishing off an opponent.

And then there were the rivalries.

If you frequented the same arcade, you'd start to recognize your toughest opponents. Some kids had unstoppable Liu Kang pressure, others could destroy with Mileena's sai throws, and everyone feared the guy who mastered Raiden's teleport-electric-fist combo.

But the best matches? Those were when you finally took down the player who had been running the arcade all night. The moment your Fatality landed perfectly on someone who had been dominating for hours?

That was the kind of gaming glory that you carried with you for days.

The Secrets That Made *Mortal Kombat II* a Legend

One of the greatest things about *Mortal Kombat II* was the sheer number of secrets hidden within it. This was before YouTube guides and internet forums, so finding these things felt like uncovering ancient knowledge.

- Babalities – Instead of brutally murdering your opponent, you could turn them into a crying baby (which, honestly, was somehow more humiliating).
- Friendships – If you wanted to mock your opponent in a more wholesome way, you could perform a non-violent, silly move like handing them a birthday cake.
- Secret Characters – Rumors spread like wildfire about how to fight hidden warriors like Smoke and Jade.
- The Infamous "Toasty!" Guy – A random floating head would pop up and yell "Toasty!", leaving everyone in the arcade wondering, *what the hell just happened?*

Every magazine, every arcade, and every kid on the playground had their own secret move list, rumored codes, or wild theories about how to unlock something crazy in *Mortal Kombat II*.

Some were real.

Some were complete nonsense made up by a kid who wanted attention.

Either way, we all spent hours trying them anyway.

Why *Mortal Kombat II* Was the Best Fighting Game of Its Time

Some might argue that *Street Fighter II* was the better overall competitive game. And sure, it had more balance, more strategic depth, and a tighter meta.

But *Mortal Kombat II*?

Mortal Kombat II was pure fun, pure arcade adrenaline, and the ultimate way to settle a rivalry in the '90s.

It had:
- 🔥 A darker, edgier aesthetic that made it feel like the forbidden fruit of gaming.
- 🔥 Characters with over-the-top movesets that made every match feel unique.
- 🔥 Finishing moves that turned a good match into an unforgettable one.
- 🔥 A sense of mystery and discovery that kept players coming back for more.

To this day, *Mortal Kombat II* holds a special place in my heart as the greatest multiplayer fighting game of its time.

It wasn't just about winning matches—it was about putting on a show, uncovering secrets, and having stories to tell long after you left the arcade.

And let's be honest:

Few things in gaming ever felt better than perfectly pulling off a Fatality with a crowd watching.

TOASTY !!!!!!!!!!!!!